Chic Shopping Paris

Chic Shopping Paris

by REBECCA PERRY MAGNIANT

PHOTOGRAPHS by ALISON HARRIS

THE LITTLE BOOKROOM
NEW YORK

© 2008 The Little Bookroom
Text © 2008 Rebecca Perry Magniant
Photographs © 2008 Alison Harris

Book Design: Louise Fili Ltd

Printed in China

Library of Congress Cataloging-in-Publication Data

Magniant, Rebecca.
Chic shopping Paris / By Rebecca Magniant ; Photography by Alison Harris.
p. cm.
Includes index.
ISBN 1-892145-57-X (alk. paper)
1. Shopping—France—Paris—Guidebooks. I. Harris, Alison. II. Title.
TX337.F82P374 2008
381.10944'361--dc22
2007040136

Published by The Little Bookroom
435 Hudson Street, 3rd Floor
New York NY 10014
editorial@littlebookroom.com
www.littlebookroom.com

10 9 8 7 6 7 5 4 3 2

A big *merci* to my parents for taking me to Paris as a teenager—without the opportunity, I never would have discovered that my teenage self disliked baguettes but loved the City of Light, and dreamed of moving here someday.

Gros bisous to my husband, for his constant encouragement and love, and for helping make his hometown my adopted one. And kisses to *la petite* Lucie, my pint-sized shopper and smiley toddler, who helps me live spontaneously.

Table of Contents

Introduction

Les Salons du Palais Royal
   Shiseido-Serge Lutens • 54

1st Arrondissement

20 sur 20 • 19
Astier de Villatte • 20
Atelier Jean Rousseau • 24
Black'Up • 27
La Boutique du Palais Royal • 29
La Bovida • 30
By Terry • 31
Causse • 32
Christian Louboutin • 33
Claudie Pierlot • 34
L'Eclaireur • 35
Egle Bespoke • 36
Gabrielle Geppert • 37
Jay Ahr • 38
Lafont • 42
Laguiole • 43
Librarie de la Mode • 44
Lydia Courteille • 45
Maison de Vacances • 46
Metal Pointu's • 48
Le Mont Saint-Michel • 49
Paule Ka • 50
La Petite Robe Noire • 51

2nd Arrondissement

Anthony Peto • 56
Pierre Corthay • 58

3rd Arrondissement

Les Archives de la Presse • 60
ba&sh • 64
Dominique Picquier • 65
Etat Libre d'Orange • 66
Isaac Reina • 69
Lemaire • 70
Matieres à réflexion • 74
Les Mille Feuilles • 75
Petite Mademoiselle • 76
Quidam de Revel • 78
Robert le Héros • 79
Swildens • 80
Titli • 81

4th Arrondissement

L'Argenterie de Turenne • 83
Au Petit Bonheur de Chance • 85
Brontibay Paris • 88
Canzi • 89

Carabosse • 90

Entrée des Fournisseurs • 93

K. Jacques • 96

Lobato • 97

Lotta & Djossou • 98

Nicole Lehmann • 99

Sandro • 100

Sentou • 101

Skeen+ • 102

Xuan-Thu Nguyen • 103

Yukiko • 104

5th Arrondissement

Côté Bastide • 107

6th Arrondissement

Adelline • 109

Alexandra Sojfer • 110

Assouline • 112

Blanc d'Ivoire • 113

Bois de Rose • 114

Cire Trudon • 115

La Compagnie de
Provence Marseille • 118

Comptoir des Cotonniers • 119

JC Martinez • 120

Karine Dupont • 121

Marie Papier • 122

Marie Puce • 126

Mis en Demure • 128

N. Villaret • 129

Nadine Delepine • 130

Les Olivades • 131

Oona L'Ourse • 132

Pierre Frey Accessories • 133

Sabbia Rosa • 135

Sabre • 136

Servane Gaxotte • 137

Tara Jarmon • 138

Vannina Vesperini • 139

7th Arrondissement

Carine Gilson • 141

Editions de Parfums Frédéric Malle • 143

Etienne Brunel • 144

Muriel Grateau • 145

Ovale • 146

Ramosport • 147

Un jour un sac • 150

8th Arrondissement

Cassegrain • 152

Gripoix • 156

Maison Calavas • 157

Repetto • 158

9th Arrondissement

Alice à Paris • 160

Anna Rivka • 161

Detaille • 162

Karine Arabian • 163

Ube Ule • 164

Woch Dom • 165

10th Arrondissement

Dante & Maria • 167

11th Arrondissement

Anne Willi • 169
Des Petits Hauts • 170
Les Fleurs • 171
Gaelle Barré • 172
Lilli Bulle • 173
Marci N'oum • 174
Philippe Roucou • 175
WallDesign • 176

12th Arrondissement

Louison • 179
Valérie Salacroux • 180

16th Arrondissement

Noël • 182
Princesse Tam-Tam • 185

18th Arrondissement

Belle de Jour • 187
Dognin Paris • 192
Ebano • 193
Gaspard de la Butte • 194
Géraldine Valluet • 195
L'Objet qui Parle • 198

Alphabetical Index

Index by Type of Shop

Introduction

PARISIANS SEEM TO BE BORN CHIC, BUT THE TRUTH IS THAT THEIR SEEMINGLY EFFORTLESS STYLE DOESN'T JUST happen. What's the secret? Well, every serious shopper starts with her *"bonnes addresses"*—a personal list of favorite shops and secret addresses. When I moved to Paris, I made it my mission to compile my own list. After a lot of wandering and exploring, I found the perfect mix: boutiques that can be counted on to have the new and trendy items each season, shops that always stock beautifully designed classics, some quirky newcomers, some established names. When some of my finds impressed the impossibly chic *belle-mère* (mother-in-law), I knew I was on to something.

At that point, it seemed natural to combine my two passions—shopping and my adopted hometown of Paris—and offer my expertise to clients. The bilingual shopping tours offered by Chic Shopping Paris give travelers a behind-the-scenes view and provide—as *Paris Notes* wrote—"even the most seasoned shopper with interesting itineraries, valuable product knowledge and in-store assistance to better enjoy the Paris shopping experience."

This book is the result of my ever-increasing knowledge of this fantastic, fashion-forward city. I've profiled the shops that I feel offer the *crème de la crème* of Paris shopping. The ones I've included are special—although many French labels are available in any major metropolis, these are ones that offer goods and/or services only available in Paris (and with many items made in France). I've also included websites when possible, to give you a sneak peek at some of the gems on offer and to help you plan your visit.

So wander, stop, admire, and enjoy the window displays and shops, and let the contents of my book inspire you to bring back a little piece of Paris in your bag.

Rebecca Perry Magniant
Paris

1ˢᵗ
Arrondissement

20 sur 20

〜∞〜

3, rue des Lavandières, 1st arr.
Telephone: 01 45 08 44 94 • Métro: Châtelet
Monday through Saturday noon to 7pm, closed Sunday

*I*F YOU ARE LOOKING FOR BRIGHT AND FUN VINTAGE JEWELRY,
CHECK OUT THIS PLAYFUL BOUTIQUE ON A SIDE STREET NEAR
Châtelet, just a short walk from the Seine. The proprietress has col-
lected vintage jewelry for decades; for twenty-three years her shop has
stocked bangles, earrings, brooches, necklaces, and more, primarily in
Bakelite, Lucite, and Galalith, a European "miracle plastic" that was
developed in the 1890s at the same time as Bakelite. The shop also has a
large array dating from the 1930s to the 1960s. A kitschy selection of col-
lectibles, such as ceramic mannequin heads, rounds out the offerings, but
those in the know come for the necklaces festooned with dangling Bakelite
cherries—new, but based on a vintage design, and exclusive to the shop.

Astier de Villatte

173, rue Saint-Honoré, 1st arr.
Telephone: 01 42 60 74 13 • Métro: Palais-Royale, Tuileries
Monday through Saturday 11am to 7:30pm, closed Sunday
astierdevillatte.com

T THE END OF RUE SAINT-HONORÉ, ASTIER DE VILLATTE IS SET APART GEOGRAPHICALLY AND CREATIVELY FROM THE rest of the big-name shops in the neighborhood. No sleek designer showroom here, rather, creaking wooden floors and a certain patina give the sense that this rustic shop has been here a lot longer than it actually has. There's a slight sense of déjà-vu: grandmother's attic, perhaps? Large wooden cabinets display the shop's signature shabby-chic ceramic tableware, in chalky, creamy white, along with dainty glassware and silverware, in matte silver or gold, that complements its style. The boutique carries a line of knitwear, as well as journals and an assortment of humorous chotchkes, such as a retro View-Master. The cheekiness of the accessories balances out the serious-ness of the gorgeous dinnerware, and it seems that in each of the rooms, a treasure is waiting to be discovered.

Atelier Jean Rousseau

9, rue Duphot, 1st arr.
Telephone: 01 47 03 05 32 • Métro: Madeleine
Monday through Saturday 10am to 7pm, closed Sunday
jean-rousseau.com

ATELIER JEAN ROUSSEAU HAS BEEN MAKING LUXURY LEATHER WATCHSTRAPS SINCE 1954. THE BRAND OPERATES ITS OWN tannery, located in Besançon, France, to insure high standards of quality control and works with allergists to insure that the watchbands are hypoallergenic. Though chang-ing watchbands is often impossible to do at home, the shop has a special clasp that can be put on a watch to make changing the strap a cinch. The idea is to have several custom bands made—alligator, lizard, silk, satin, and shark are among the choices—to vary a watch's look. (The company states that it is deeply committed to the environment and protection of endangered species. All skins have clearly identified origins and the company has im-posed on itself bans on using certain skins that are still commonly used

in the fashion industry.) The boutique, located on a side street off of rue Saint-Honoré, offers more than one hundred different color choices of watch bands; belts, wallets, card holders, and other leather goods can also be custom ordered in colors and patterns to suit your whimsy.

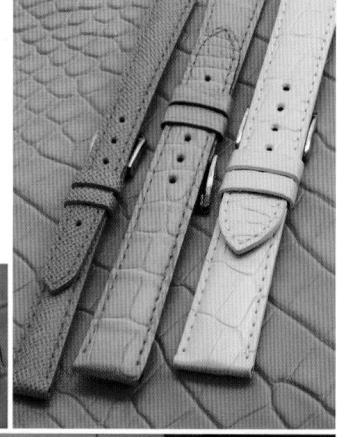

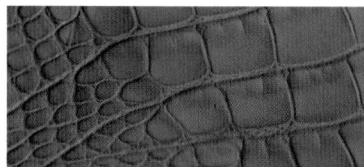

Black' Up

ommo

12, rue de Turbigo, 1nd arr.
Telephone: 01 42 21 36 32 • Métro: Etienne Marcel
Monday through Saturday 10:30am to 7:30pm, closed Sunday
blackup.com

FABRICE MAHABO'S PROFESSIONAL COSMETICS LINE, CREATED IN 1999, IS THE FIRST FRENCH BRAND CREATED BY A MAKEUP ARTIST for women of all ethnicities. Quality pigments are mixed in a variety of colors for different skin tones, and textures that range from light to long-lasting, depending on your skin's needs. The skincare line is a newer addition to the brand, with all the products based on white lily extracts, which works as both a softener and as an astringent. Stepping into the boutique, the red, black, and white contemporary design scheme looks a bit like a photography gallery, a bit like a makeup studio. No boutiques are stateside at the moment, as the line is limited to use by professionals in the U.S., but fans can order online. With an appointment, the space can be booked for a makeup lesson with friends.

La Boutique du Palais Royal

9, rue de Beaujolais. 1st arr.
Telephone: 01 42 60 08 22 • Métro: Palais-Royal
Monday through Saturday 10:30am to 7pm, closed Sunday

TUCKED AWAY AT THE BACK OF THE PALAIS-ROYAL, LA BOUTIQUE SPE-
CIALIZES IN TWO FRENCH-MADE TOY LINES—VILAC AND PETITCOLLIN.
Vilac has been making toys since 1911 in the Jura district of France.
The brightly colored wooden toys, with a shiny, lacquer-like finish, are still great gifts today. Little cars to push and pull, boats for sailing in the Luxembourg gardens, blocks, puppet theaters, wooden tricycles, puzzles, dominoes, and cute child-size umbrellas—the shop seems to have a gift for every age. Petitcollin is the maker of the quintessential French baby doll, which now comes in a wide range of sizes and ethnicities, sporting clothing from a 60s swing dress to a classic French beret. The "Chic de Paris" line of dolls is a favorite that will please *petites filles* of all ages.

La Bovida

36, rue Montmartre, 1st arr.
Telephone: 01 42 36 09 99 • Métro: Etienne Marcel
Monday through Friday 9am to 7pm, Saturday 10am to 7pm, closed Sunday

NEAR THE FORMER FOOD MARKETS AT LES HALLES, LA BOVIDA IS ONE OF THE MORE UPSCALE RESTAURANT SUPPLY STORES IN THE area. The imposing two-story corner shop stocks professional kitchen equipment but sells to individuals as well. The business, founded in 1921, carries more than 8,000 products. This is a great stop for gourmet gifts such as a mandolin or a bistro-type mustard set for the table. As well as all sorts of cooking equipment and tabletop items, you'll find a huge selection of bulk spices and canned specialty items (check out the La Bovida *herbes aromatiques pour grillades*, a mix of *herbes de Provence* especially for grilling, or perhaps a jar of white truffles). La Bovida isn't as frenzied as their famous neighbor down the street, Dehellerin, and the friendly, reliable staff is willing to help you find just what you need to satisfy your gourmet desires.

By Terry

36, Passage Vero Dodat, 1st arr.
Telephone: 01 44 76 00 76 • Métro: Louvre-Rivoli
Monday through Saturday 10:30am to 7pm, closed Sunday
byterry.com

FORMER CREATIVE DIRECTOR AT YSL, TERRY DE GUNZBURG KNOWS A THING OR TWO ABOUT WHAT MAKES FASHIONISTAS HAPPY. ONE way is with high-quality French-made makeup. The entire line of her *prêt-à-porter* collection of luxurious cosmetics and skincare can be found here in her sophisticated flagship shop at the end of this elegant nineteenth-century covered arcade. Make an appointment for a personalized makeup lesson (165 euros), or purchase a beauty case that can be filled to your specifications and replenished with the products. The shop also features a small collection of rotating home decor *objets* for sale, such as handpainted Limoges, crystal glasses, and Terry's signature candles. Further inside the *passage* at Number 21 is de Gunzburg's haute couture shop, Haute Couleur. Look for the giant test tubes filled with a rainbow of pigments. This is the place to come for a custom-made lipstick or custom-blended foundation, a service exclusively available at this location. The prices for this service can be close to that of a haute couture gown, and it is by appointment only, *bien sûr*.

Causse

12, rue de Castiglione, 1st arr.
Telephone: 01 49 26 91 43 • Métro: Tuileries
Monday through Saturday 10:30am to 2pm, 2:30pm to 7pm, closed Sunday
causse-gantier.fr

FOR MORE THAN 115 YEARS, THE MAISON CAUSSE HAS BEEN PRO-
DUCING REFINED, HANDMADE GLOVES IN THE TOWN OF MILLAU,
France. September 2007 marked the opening of their first Parisian
boutique, a sleek and polished armoire-like space designed by architect
Jean-Michel Wilmotte, with floor-to-ceiling drawers full of their star
product. Fine materials such as lamb, stag, and ostrich are made into
second skins to wear on your hands. The brand, which has enjoyed a
renaissance with the addition of two artistic directors in 2003, has always
had couture houses among its clients. The exquisite detailing—fur,
sequins, lace, and buckles—have made loyal clients of Karl Lagerfeld and
other designers. The line contains town, evening, and sportswear models
for both men and women.

Christian Louboutin

19, rue Jean-Jacques Rousseau, 1st arr.
Telephone: 01 42 36 05 31 • Métro: Louvre-Rivoli, Palais-Royale
Monday through Saturday 10:30am to 7pm, closed Sunday
christianlouboutin.fr

OUSED IN A FORMER *IMPRIMERIE* (PRINT SHOP) IN ONE OF THE LOVELY OLD NINETEENTH-CENTURY PASSAGEWAYS, CHRISTIAN Louboutin's headquarters entices you with its legendary red leather-soled shoes. The crimson carpet and the scarlet velvet mannequin further emphasize that this is a place where luxe reigns and all of the creations are worthy of fashion royalty. Each of the cubbyholes in the window and along the shop wall display a precious pair of *chaussures*, from the tallest stilettos to the flattest flats and several styles in between. If you can't find the perfect pair in stock, the shop also offers—only in Paris at this location—a *sur mesure* service. Pick the style and the color, and you can have your custom pair made and sent to you.

Claudie Pierlot

1, rue Montmartre, 1st arr.
Telephone: 01 42 21 38 38 • Métro: Etienne Marcel
Monday through Friday 10:30am to 7pm
Saturday 10:30am to 7:30pm, closed Sunday
claudiepierlot.com

IF YOU ARE ACHING FOR THE GROWN-UP GAMINE LOOK, LOOK NO FURTHER THAN CLAUDIE PIERLOT'S SIMPLE, SWEET BOUTIQUE. French-born Pierlot worked in knitwear and as a stylist for the Printemps department store before launching her own line. Her fresh take on casual clothing for every day is popular with all ages, although the cheeky but demure slim styles look best on those with svelte figures. Pierlot strives for well-cut shapes that aren't overly trendy and have a certain timelessness to them. Striped A-line sheaths, swingy trench coats, and blouses with Peter Pan collars: the look is "Breakfast at Tiffany's" in Paris. The colorful separates often have details such as stripes, buttons, and bows, but never used in a saccharine way—these are looks that work in the city as well as on holiday.

L'Éclaireur

10, rue Herold, 1st arr.
Telephone: 01 40 41 09 89 • Métro: Louvre-Rivoli, Etienne Marcel
Monday through Saturday 11am to 7pm, closed Sunday
leclaireur.com

ONE OF THE HOTTEST TRENDSETTING BOUTIQUES SINCE IT WAS FOUNDED IN 1980, L'ECLAIREUR ("THE SCOUT") OFFERS UP A DOSE of what's next before it's a has-been. The shop's renown grew as it expanded to different chic locations across the city, offering designs by Philippe Starck and Jean Nouvel alongside hot fashion labels such as Alexander McQueen, Haute, and Costume National. Owners Martine and Armand Hadida pride themselves on offering collections from a variety of designers as well as items that are exclusive to their boutiques. The atmosphere is always eclectic with a mix of modern and antique decor; the multilingual staff are interesting and friendly. Both Lenny Kravitz and John Galliano have stopped by and have cited L'Eclaireur as their favorite Parisian stop for clothing. The rue Herold shop, hidden from street view and with a door that is opened only after ringing the bell, houses a women's line, menswear, and recently added furniture and objects by the Dutch designer Piet Hein Eek. The boutique at 8, rue Boissy d'Anglas in the eighth arrondissement also recently opened a restaurant—the ultimate in *branché* (trendy) dining.

Eglé Bespoke

26, rue du Mont Thabor, 1st arr.
Telephone: 01 44 15 98 31 • Métro: Tuileries
Monday through Saturday 11am to 7pm, closed Sunday
eglebespoke.com

PHILIPPE LE BLAN AND RÉGIS DECOUR STARTED THEIR OWN BRAND AFTER IDENTIFYING A NEED FOR QUALITY SHIRTS WITHOUT THE stuffiness associated with traditional custom tailoring. The pair created Eglé Bespoke in 2005, starting with a private showroom, then opening a shop near the chic place Vendôme. The stylish boutique has a look that appeals to the modern-day dandy with black-and-white printed floral wallpaper and a black crystal chandelier. The shirts, starting at 119 euros, are *haute mesure*, a combination of haute couture (read: elegance) and *sur mesure* (think: quality). There are more than 2,000 fabric choices, twelve different collar and cuff styles, and other personalization options including monogramming in two colors to give a modern effect or silk lining the cuffs. Eglé Bespoke claims to be the only shirtmaker that offers engraved buttons for their shirts; the small white disks come from the South American corozo nut and may be incised with up to twenty-four characters. Boxer shorts, to match or contrast with the shirts, can also be custom ordered, and accessories such as cuff links, ties, belts, and handkerchiefs are on hand to complete the look. Jeans for both women and men can be made to order as well, in a variety of cuts and washes, starting at 189 euros.

Gabrielle Geppert

31 & 34, Galerie de Montpensier, 1st arr.
Telephone: 01 42 61 53 52 • Métro: Palais-Royale
Monday through Saturday 10:30am to 8pm, closed Sunday
gabriellegeppert.com

IN HER LUMINOUS ALL-WHITE BOUTIQUE, GABRIELLE GEPPERT SELLS A MOSAIC OF COLORFUL VINTAGE CLOTHING AND ACCESSORIES. From geometric jewelry from the 1970s that looks oh-so-modern again (think Pierre Cardin, Courrèges, big chunky bangles) to dainty turn-of-the-century evening bags, Geppert has it. Drawers open to reveal vintage sunglasses; long necklaces dangle from mirrors above racks of premium vintage frocks. The range of items date mainly from the 1930s and 40s to the modern day. If you are looking for a special party dress or a certain accessory, Geppert will be happy to use her talent as a stylist to assist you. Her second shop, just a few doors down, is open by appointment only, and showcases some of her latest treasures. Fans include Betsey Johnson and gal pal of Geppert's neighbor Monsieur Jacobs, Sofia Coppola.

Jay Ahr

2-4, rue du 29 Juillet, 1st arr.
Telephone: 01 42 96 95 23 • Métro: Tuileries
Monday through Saturday 11am to 7pm, closed Sunday
jayahr.com

JONATHAN RISS, THE SON OF BELGIAN DESIGNER JOHANNE RISS, OPENED THIS BOUTIQUE WHICH IS QUICKLY BECOMING *THE* PARISIAN address for the ultimate in red carpet dresses. The shop's name is a play on his initials; the setting is neo-baroque, with clean lines and a touch of romanticism, just like the frocks. The dresses, in luxurious fabrics and sensual shapes, flatter the figure: both short jersey wrap dresses and gowns, strapless and backless, mostly in deep solid colors, with a few well-chosen prints (panther, polka dots) mixed in. The long versions could easily go to Cannes, the short ones to a night out in Ibiza or dinner in Paris—everything is extremely comfortable and body conscious, with just a bit of a rock 'n' roll vibe. Jay Ahr also designs wedding dresses and jewelery—check out the collection of diamond earrings, which offers seven gorgeous pairs, one for each day.

Lafont

2, rue Duphot, 1st arr.
Telephone: 01 42 60 01 02 • Métro: Madeleine
Monday 10:30am to 1:30pm, 2:30pm to 7pm, Tuesday through Friday
10:30am to 7pm, Saturday 11am to 7pm, closed Sunday
lafont.com

LUXURY EYEGLASS BRAND LAFONT WAS ESTABLISHED IN 1923 BY THE GRANDFATHER OF CURRENT PROPRIETOR PHILIPPE LAFONT. PHILIPPE expanded the business in 1979 and partnered with his wife Laurence, a designer, to overhaul the look of the line. Now known worldwide for their quality frames, entirely made in the Jura region of France, the Lafonts present two new collections a year for men, women, and children, in both soft earthy tones and bright-brights along with panther prints and polka dots. Styles range from traditional to avant garde limited editions designed by Laurence. Part of the charm of the brand is that each of their several olive green Paris shops is welcoming and intimate, with fun, seasonal window displays. The rue Duphot address is a quaint mini-building on the corner of rue Saint-Honoré, a discreet and personal presence in the midst of all the glittery fashion houses nearby.

Laguiole

1, place Sainte Opportune, 1st arr.
Telephone: 01 40 28 09 42 • Métro: Châtelet
Tuesday through Saturday 10:30am to 1:15pm, noon to 7pm • closed Sunday
forge-de-laguiole.com

THE HISTORY OF LAGUIOLE KNIVES BEGINS IN 1829 IN THE MASSIF CENTRAL REGION OF FRANCE WHERE THE FIRST KNIFE WAS MADE IN steel with handles fashioned from local steer horns. This instantly popular folding knife was perfected over the years, with the later addition of a corkscrew. Over time, the brand all but fell into obscurity until it was reestablished in the 1980s. In 1987, Philippe Starck designed the new factory, and the brand quickly attained the status of a modern luxury item. The boutiques, also designed by Starck, house metal cases filled with knives displayed as if they were fine jewelry. The knives are made in several different types of steel, some that develop a patina over time, some with a moiré appearance; handles are horn, bone, exotic wood, aluminum, or carbon fiber. Chic models by Sonia Rykiel (in her signature red and black), Hermès (leather and steel), and Courrèges (with neon acrylic handles) have made these items popular with style-conscious buyers as well as hunters and chefs. The symbol of Laguiole, the bee, appears on the base of each blade, establishing its authenticity.

Librarie de la Mode

22, rue Pierre Lescot, 1st arr.
Telephone: 01 40 13 81 50 • Métro: Etienne Marcel
Monday through Friday 9am to 7pm, Saturday 10am to 6pm, closed Sunday
modeinfo.com

SINCE JANUARY 2007, FASHION FANS HAVE A NEW REFERENCE POINT IN PARIS FOR INSTANT INSPIRATION. NOT FAR FROM THE CENTRE Pompidou museum, this calm, vast space, designed for both pros and novices alike, contains more than 1,000 titles on fashion, architecture and design. Highly specialized magazines in dozens of languages are available along with sleek books on subjects like couture, trend-spotting, and lifestyle, all in a glam *librarie*. The staff will help you seek out exactly what you need, patiently explaining that, *bien sûr*, wallpaper is making a comeback and shag rugs are so *démodé*.

Lydia Courteille

231, rue Saint-Honore, 1st arr.
Telephone: 01 42 61 11 71 • Métro: Tuileries
Monday through Saturday 10:30am to 6:30pm and by appointment

IF YOU ARE WALKING DOWN RUE SAINT-HONORÉ INDULGING IN SOME *LECHE VITRINES* (THE FRENCH TERM FOR WINDOW SHOP-ping—literally, "window licking"), you'll discover this tiny blue velvet-lined boutique that houses Lydia Courteille's stunning jewelry collection. Inside the minuscule shop decorated with Venetian mirrors and antique screens, cases are filled with extraordinary cameos, brooches, tiaras, earrings, and more. Courteille carries her own line as well as antique jewelry and vintage pieces from Cartier, Boucheron, and other prestigious houses. In her own designs, Courteille uses large gemstones "with personality" and reworks old pieces for today's modern tastes. Courteille's craftsmanship and inventiveness are apparent in items such as a gorgeous crown ring made of lacy gold and diamonds, an amusing monkey ring, a butterfly pendant with uncut diamonds and sapphires, and giant hoops festooned with twenty-some opals. Her imaginative take on bijoux appeals to posh and famous clients as well as artists and collectors.

Maison de Vacances

63-64, Galerie de Montpensier, 1st arr.
Telephone: 01 47 03 99 74 • Métro: Palais-Royale
Tuesday through Saturday 11am to 2pm, 2:30pm to 7pm, closed Sunday
maisondevacances.com

THIS PALAIS-ROYALE BOUTIQUE FEELS MODERN AND CLEAN, A REFRESHING CONTRAST TO THE ANCIENT ARCADES OVERHEAD. THE items here, made by a husband-and-wife team, offer a masculine and feminine take on home decor. Like a fashion house, the boutique presents two collections a year, playing on the latest colors and textile trends, using both strong brights and neutrals in a wide array of home accessories— bags, throws, sophisticated lounge-wear, furry slippers, and the signature pillows inscribed with the word "love." There is an array of throw pillows in countless materials— metallic leather, fur, knits, silks—all with a natural linen backing, which allows one to play with the arrangement by flipping over the pillows for a different look. Items can also be custom made.

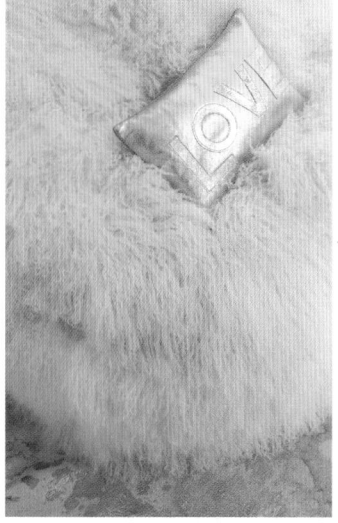

Metal Pointu's

13, rue du Jour, 1st arr.
Telephone: 01 42 33 51 52 • Métro: Les Halles
Monday through Saturday 10:30am to 2pm, 3pm to 7pm, closed Sunday
metalpointus.com

SITUATED IN THE SHADOW OF SAINT-EUSTACHE, THE BOUTIQUE/ATELIER METAL POINTU'S HAS BEEN CREATING JEWELRY FOR FOURteen years. Designer Bernard Bounic uses brushed metal, bronze, and pewter, along with glass and Swarovski crystals. The result is slightly edgy, slightly rock 'n' roll, with a bit of an ethnic influence. Two collections are produced each year, although much of the store's offerings are basic items that are always available. At first glance, the shop, with its large metal display tables and flourescent accents, seems to appeal to a young clientele, but in fact many of the pieces on offer are classically inspired and easily integrated into a traditional wardrobe. The wide stretch bracelets of little bars of pewter or bronze beads are an easy-to-wear statement piece; or, throw on skinny brushed-metal bangles or a medallion necklace for an everyday look. The inexpensive prices make these pieces an attractive gift, as does the "Made in Paris" label.

Le Mont Saint-Michel

29, rue du Jour, 1st arr.
Telephone: 01 53 40 80 44 • Métro: Les Halles, Etienne Marcel
Monday 12:30pm to 7pm• Tuesday through Saturday
11am to 2pm, 3pm to 7pm, closed Sunday
lemontsaintmichel.fr

LE MONT SAINT-MICHEL, FOUNDED IN 1913, WAS ORIGINALLY A COM-
PANY KNOWN FOR WORKERS' CLOTHING: COTTON MOLESKIN WORK
coats and firemen's uniforms. The brand was purchased in 1999
by Alexander Milan, whose family's business was the manufacturing of
knitwear. Inspired by knits from the family archives from the 50s and
60s, he reinvented Le Mont Saint-Michel by creating a line of fashionable
women's, men's, and children's clothing. The specialty is knitwear in fine
materials (cotton, alpaca, cashmere, merino), often with fun retro twists
on classics like the vintage tennis sweater. Alongside the brightly colored
sweaters, tanks, scarves, mittens, funky little shorts, and flowing dresses,
you'll find tote bags with the vintage company logo, a new line of shoes,
and reissued editions of the original work coats. The children's collection
is made up of retro-style cardigans, mini-capes, and bonnets, in the school-
uniform-gone-modern look that the brand is known for. No dark colors or
endless racks of black clothing here—everything is bright and fun, with
that extra *"detail qui tue"* (killer detail).

Paule Ka

223, rue Saint-Honoré, 1st arr.
Telephone: 01 42 97 57 06 • Métro: Tuileries
Monday through Saturday 10:30am to 7pm, closed Sunday
pauleka.com

FOR MANY A PARISIENNE, PAULE KA SIGNIFIES ELEGANCE AND DISCREET LUXURY. THE LINE, STARTED IN 1987 BY SERGE Cajfinger, is full of chic, wearable separates that are urban and modern, yet classic enough to wear year after year. Cajfinger's designs reflect the self-confidence and elegance of Jacqueline Kennedy Onassis, Audrey Hepburn, and Grace Kelly, along with his own mix of French and Brazilian cultures. The result: classic little dresses with an extra-flirty hem, short jackets that are tailored just so, and other items that mix and match for a timeless, graceful look. The brand caters to all occasions with its citywear suits and separates, a casual cruise line, and cocktail dresses. The twentieth anniversary of the brand was celebrated in 2007 with the opening of this flagship boutique on the rue Saint-Honoré. Be sure to check out the 223 bag, the label's new signature purse, named after its new address.

La Petite Robe Noire

Galerie de Valois, 1st arr.
) 15 01 04 • Métro: Palais-Royale
Saturday 11am to 7pm, closed Sunday
didierludot.com

IDDEN UNDER THE ARCADES IN THE PALAIS ROYALE, DIDIER LUDOT'S SECOND BOUTIQUE (THE FIRST IS HIS EPONYMOUS vintage shop across the garden), focuses on the one item in a woman's closet that never seems to go out of fashion—the little black dress. The boutique's red carpet and oversized red hanging lampshades make you feel as if you have stepped out to your own carpet-worthy event when you try on one of his creations. The shop originally started with vintage versions of the little black dress, and then Ludot started making his own designs, with names like Miami, Capri, and St. Tropez. The shop designs thirteen new dresses a year, along with one bolero and one coat. A few pairs of select vintage shoes perched under glass cloches and vintage furs on display in winter round out the collection.

Les Salons du Palais Royal Shiseido-Serge Lutens

142, Galerie de Valois, 1st arr.
Telephone: 01 49 27 09 09 • Métro: Palais-Royal
Monday through Saturday 10am to 7pm, closed Sunday
salons-shiseido.com

FROM THE OUTSIDE, LES SALONS DU PALAIS ROYAL SHISEIDO APPEARS CLOSED AND SOMEHOW PRIVATE, BUT AS YOU WALK BY, the door automatically opens as if by magic, inviting you to enter. The dark-mauve-and-black boutique sells fragrances by Serge Lutens, who opened it in 1992 to sell his own scents. In 2000, his collaboration with Shiseido led to an expanded collection. Half of the creative, sophisticated fragrances sold in this cozy, jewel-box boutique are exclusive to this location—look for the round bottles with scents such as Mandarine-Mandarin, Iris Silver Mist, Encens et Lavande, Borneo 1834, Un Lys, and Bois et Fruits, which are sold nowhere else in the world. All are 75-ml bottles and cost 100 euros. (The other Lutens scents that are sold here—the ones in the rectangular bottles—are also available in the U.S.) For an extra fee, you can add your initials or the name of your loved one to the label, engraved or enameled in black, an oh-so-chic touch. During the holidays, check out the limited editions—each Christmas (since 1996), Lutens has released an engraved original bottle, in an edition of thirty.

2nd
Arrondissement

Anthony Peto

56, rue Tiquetonne, 2nd arr.
Telephone: 01 40 26 60 68 • Métro: Etienne Marcel
Monday through Saturday 11am to 7pm, closed Sunday
anthonypeto.com

INSIDE THE CHERRY-RED BOUTIQUE OF ANTHONY PETO, YOU'LL FIND A WORLD OF HATS, FROM THE MELON HAT TO THE COWBOY, to the Panama and the beret. The hats are unisex and slightly whimsical, with a certain sense of style and fun. Before going out on his own to design a men's line, Peto originally collaborated on a women's hat collection with Marie Mercie (her boutique for women is at 23, rue Saint-Sulpice in the sixth arrondissement). The woman's line quickly became the most famous hat line in France, and in 1992, Peto started his line. Both lines offer high-quality, handmade hats with a lot of personality. The unisex *chapeaux*, in straw for summer and felt for winter, are worn by the diverse likes of Yoko Ono, Nicolas Cage, and Justin Timberlake.

Pierre Corthay

1, rue Volney, 2nd arr.
Telephone: 01 42 61 08 89 • Métro: Madeleine
Monday through Friday 9:30am to 7pm• Saturday 10:30am to 12:30pm,
2:30pm to 7pm, closed Sunday
corthay.fr

CORTHAY STARTED HIS CAREER AT THE YOUNG AGE OF SIXTEEN, LEARNING TO BE A MASTER COBBLER. AFTER WORKING FOR JOHN Lobb and Berluti, Corthay opened his first shop in 1990 near the Place Vendôme to showcase his line of men's shoes, first offering a bespoke service and then branching out with ready to wear. To reach the sales area at Corthay, you must pass through the workshop, which creates an intimate experience between the craftsman and the client. The *prêt* line has clever names such as Oedipus Rex, with bright trim outlining the shoe, and Schizo, with blocks of different colors that, Corthay says, are meant to represent different states of mind. All are made out of the finest leathers and hand-stitched, as is the new line of small leather goods (belts, wallets). The bespoke shoes, such as the Bosphore (straw, calf leather and natural crocodile) are true works of art.

3rd
Arrondissement

Les Archives de la Presse

51, rue des Archives, 3rd arr.
Telephone: 01 42 72 63 93 • Métro: Hôtel de Ville, Filles du Calvaire
Monday through Friday 10:30am to 7pm
Saturday 2pm to 7pm, closed Sunday
lesarchivesdelapresse.com

L OCATED NEAR THE NATIONAL ARCHIVES, LES ARCHIVES DE LA PRESSE IS A TREASURE TROVE OF ALL KINDS OF PRINTED MATTER — MAGAZINES, books, posters, etc. The shop specializes in magazines from the nineteenth century to the present. If you are looking for inspiration from an old *journal* filled with illustrations of Balenciaga garments or for a pretty copy of *La Vie Parisienne* from the 1930s to frame, or even a vintage comic book, this is the place. A huge assortment awaits, so arrive with some idea of what you are looking for—or plan to spend a while doing some serious browsing. While slightly dusty and musty inside, the shop staff knows the inventory, and has one of the largest collections of periodicals in the city.

CHASSE

NOTRE CORPS, NOUS MÊMES

disette 193

1939

MONOGRAPHIE

Château de Bagatelle

au Bois de Boulogne, près Paris

Ancienne Propriété de Sir Richard WALLACE

Propriété actuelle de la Ville de Paris

INTÉRIEURS ET EXTÉRIEURS

Style Louis XVI

Good
Housekeep

CRONI

ba & sh

⟨∞⟩

22, rue des Francs Bourgeois, 3rd arr.
Telephone: 01 42 78 55 10 • Métro: Saint-Paul
Monday through Saturday 11am to 7:30pm, Sunday 1pm to 7pm
ba-sh.com

FRIENDS SINCE CHILDHOOD, BARBARA BOCCARA AND SHARON KRIEF CREATED, IN 2003, A FASHION LINE THAT REFLECTS THE TYPE of clothing they wanted to wear every day. The result is modern, feminine, a bit edgy, and very French. The duo focuses on clothing in natural fabrics such as cashmere, silk, and fine cotton and also carries their own line of accessories. The boutique, like the clothing, is simple and chic—it's no surprise Cameron Diaz and French fave Charlotte Gainsbourg are among its fans. This line's swingy little leather jackets, chic tops that pair perfectly with jeans, and short little tunic dresses have quickly become Parisienne staples. The line will be introduced in the U.S. in summer 2008.

Dominique Picquier

10, rue Charlot, 3rd arr.
Telephone: 01 42 72 23 32 • Métro: Saint-Sebastien-Froissart
Monday through Friday 10am to 1pm, 2pm to 7pm
Saturday 2:30pm to 7pm, closed Sunday
dominiquepicquier.com

TEXTILE DESIGNER DOMINIQUE PICQUIER LIKES THE SHAPES OF FLOWERS AND LEAVES, THE LIGHTNESS OF BAMBOO AND SILK, THE SHADOWS AND movement of trees; these are themes you will see over and over again in her stunning, modern home-decorating fabrics. Using natural motifs and rich colors such as red, black, and khaki green, her signature color, Picquier creates materials with graphic images that pop, and yet are classic enough to fit with traditional decor. You'll find red poppies on a beige background, an "X-ray" of mimosa flowers, swirling water patterns, and windblown vines. Her designs are woven in Normandy, in a blend of linen and cotton, and then printed in Lyon. The robust, long-lasting fabric has slight irregularities that give it character and authenticity. Gingko leaves, orchids, and trees dance across tote bags, wallets, pillows, and fabric by the meter. The boutique also offers drapery and upholstery services.

Etat Libre d'Orange

69, rue des Archives, 3rd arr.
Telephone: 01 42 78 30 09 • Métro: Temple
Tuesday through Saturday noon to 7:30pm, closed Sunday, Monday
etatlibredorange.com

T HE DARK GRAY AWNINGS ON THIS CORNER BOUTIQUE MAKE IT
STAND OUT AGAINST ITS BLAND NEIGHBORS, BUT ALSO SEEM TO HELP
conceal the risqué nature of what is happening inside—this shop is a
perfumery, but definitely not your mother's. Creator Etienne de Swardt,
the nose behind the famous Oh! My
Dog scent from a few years back,
invites you into an all-black interior,
set off with a fuchsia rug. The brand's
slogan is *"Vive le parfum, parfum est
mort!"* (Long live perfume, perfume
is dead!), which hints at the rebel-
lious nature of this shop. Some names
are naughty, others border on the
ridiculous—*"Vraie Blonde"* (Real
Blonde) to *"Je suis un Homme"* (I am
a man) to *"Putain des Palaces"* (Palace
Whore) and *"Nombril Immense"*
(Immense Bellybutton). One of the
perfumes is even called *"Rien,"* created so that the wearer could answer

"Nothing" when asked what she is wearing. Etat Libre d'Orange bottles have bright, graphic logos that pop, much like the fragrance names; the authentic scents are designed for those looking for originality. Not for wallflowers, this is fragrance with fresh, funky spirit. And if the scents don't appeal, check out the off-color, cheeky books on everything from Leonardo da Vinci to plastic surgery.

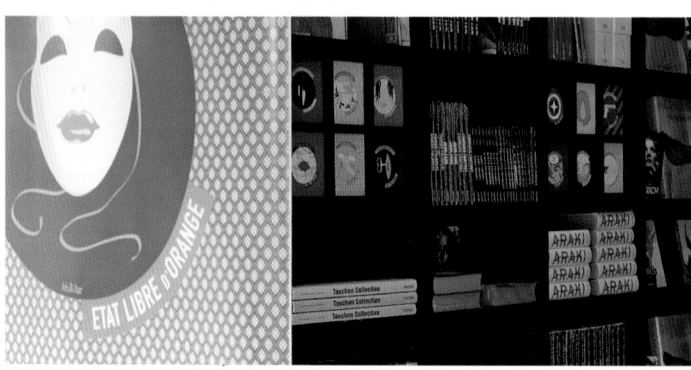

Isaac Reina

◦◦◦◦

38, rue de Sévigné, 3rd arr.
Telephone: 01 42 78 81 95 • Métro: Saint-Paul
Tuesday through Saturday 11am to 7:30pm, closed Sunday, Monday
isaacreina.com

IN THIS MINIMALIST SHOP THAT HAS THE AIR OF AN ARCHITEC-
TURAL FIRM, BARCELONA-BORN ISSAC REINA CREATES STRUCTURED
leather goods for men and women. The simple shapes are laid on
long wooden counters and include leather purses and bags, pouches, small
wallets, portfolios, weekend bags, and large briefcases. No funky patterns
or frilly shapes here, just pure, minimal designs that are practical and
functional in a range of neutral colors such as white, natural, and black.
Reina began his career in menswear and worked in design at Hermès
before setting off on his own, inspired by minimalist designers like Jasper
Morrison and Jean Prouvé. He strives to make the lines of his bags look
almost industrial, while the fine materials and quality show off their
handmade qualities. His elegant pieces are named only with a model
number, in keeping with the graphic design theme.

Lemaire

~~~

28, rue de Poitou, 3rd arr.
Telephone: 01 44 78 00 09 • Métro: Filles du Calvaire
Monday through Saturday 11am to 7:30pm, closed Sunday
lemairestyle.com

OCCUPYING A LARGE FORMER PHARMACY IN THE UP-AND-COMING HAUTE MARAIS (UPPER MARAIS) NEIGHBORHOOD, LEMAIRE AND ITS black façade attract curious passersbys with an elegant but forbidding exterior. Inside, the white gold-faceted ceiling hangs over an interior decor of hi-tech mixed with vintage that hints at the mélange of styles

influencing Lemaire's menswear. Christophe Lemaire started his career as an intern at YSL, then as a design assistant at Christian Lacroix, and also as a DJ, which explains the stylish rock 'n' roll vibe throughout his clothing line. In 2000, he also became the creative director for Lacoste. His namesake lines (one for men, one for women, and one unisex) are each divided into a sportswear-focused outdoor line and one of more structured pieces such as suits, coats, and basics. The look has an elegant, modern-day Ziggy Stardust vibe, for those who like an offbeat, dandified look.

Matières à réflexion

19, rue de Poitou, 3rd arr.
Telephone: 01 42 72 16 31 • Métro: Saint-Sebastien-Froissart
Tuesday through Saturday noon to 7pm, Sunday 3pm to 7pm
matieresareflexion.com

MATIÈRES À RÉFLEXION USES VINTAGE LEATHER JACKETS AS RAW MATERIAL TO MAKE NEW BAGS—THE ULTIMATE IN recycling. Styles range from clutches to oversized totes, all soft and lightweight, each a numbered *piece unique* because it retains the details of the jacket it was made from—pleats, pockets, studs, leather buttons. All are handmade (you can see creators Laetitia and Cyrille at work in their atelier in the boutique). The unisex MàR UrbanBag line, created for men but also used by women, is practical and more structured than the original line, but with the hallmark focus on detail. This line uses either leather alone or mixed with vintage army jacket material. The boutique also offers a made-to-measure service—bring in an outdated jacket (maybe one found scrounging around the *puces*), pick a style, and a bag can be made in as few as two days. The couple also supports other young designers by carrying small French brands of bijoux (Adeline Cacheux, Eva Gozlan) and *prêt* (Charlotte Sometime, Karine Jean) in their boutique.

Les Mille Feuilles

2, rue Rambuteau, 3rd arr.
Telephone: 01 42 78 32 93 • Métro: Rambuteau
Monday 2pm to 7pm, Tuesday through Saturday
10am to 1pm, 2pm to 7pm, closed Sunday
les-mille-feuilles.com

IF YOU ARE LOOKING FOR A TRULY INTERESTING OBJET, OR PERHAPS JUST SOME INSIGHT INTO THE FRENCH *ART DE VIVRE*, LOOK NO further than Les Milles Feuilles ("a thousand leaves"). The owner wants the shop to remain "unique and inimitable," a goal which he pursues with eclectic styling that combines fanciful displays of home accessories with floral decoration. The shop follows mostly traditional themes, but in a creative, innovative way. Those in the know come here to snatch up toile de Jouy-printed lampshades, sunburst mirrors, vases, small paintings and statues (some of which are actual antiques, some reproductions). Or, you might happen on to such gems as a hand-blown paperweight or a cameo-incrusted obelisk. In short, if you can't make it to the *puces* and want to fake it or if you simply need a *soupçon* of French good taste, come here.

Petite Mademoiselle

20, rue du Pont aux Choux, 3rd arr.
Telephone: 01 42 93 43 06 • Métro: Saint-Sebastien-Froissart
Monday through Saturday 10am to 7pm, closed Sunday

PETITE MADEMOISELLE'S FIRST SHOP, IN THE UP-AND-COMING HAUTE MARAIS NEIGHBORHOOD, LOOKS LIKE A CLOSET overflowing with girly accessories. The boutique, wallpapered in a hot pink flowered pattern, is filled with mirrors and lamps from the flea market; the ceiling dangles with retro suspension lamps. Celine Faraud

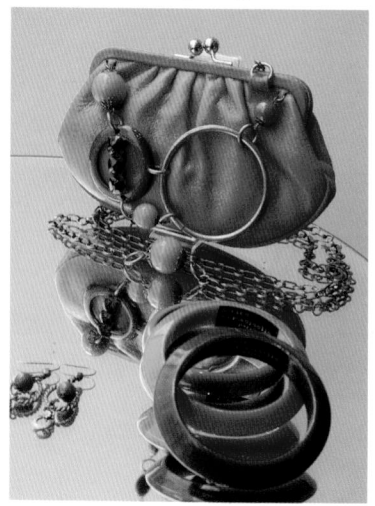

designs two collections a year, created in her atelier in the basement of the shop. Well-known for long *sautoir* necklaces, already a hit in Japan, she mixes materials such as pearls, semi-precious stones, leather, or bits of fabric like silk and wool. Her creations are suspended from racks on the walls, dangling from mannequins, and displayed on little tables. She also makes headbands and small bags and will create custom items on request. If you like bows, baubles, and chains, Faraud's designs are for you.

Quidam de Revel

24-26, rue de Poitou, 3rd arr.
Telephone: 01 42 71 37 07 • Metro: Saint-Sebastien-Froissart
Tuesday through Saturday 2pm to 7:30pm, closed Sunday
quidam-de-revel.com

STOP BY QUIDAM DE REVEL TO FIND IMPECCABLE TREASURES, COL-LECTED BY HUSBAND AND WIFE TEAM: EMMANUELLE, AN ART historian, and Philippe, an antiquarian. Each piece is selected with their combined expert knowledge, and must be particularly daring in some way. Jewelry, clothes, accessories, bags, and interesting *objets* from the 1920s to the 1970s are on hand in each of their two boutiques. No. 24 is an ever-changing space open to the public, and no. 26 is by appointment only for rentals and consulting. The shops carry a mix of haute couture and *prêt* (Roger Vivier, Chanel, Pucci, Lanvin, and more) and jewelry from the eighteenth century onward (Vautrin, Georg Jensen, and Boucheron, among others), making this an important stop on the vintage circuit for novices and fashion pros alike.

Robert le Héros

13, rue de Saintonge, 3rd arr.
Telephone: 01 44 59 33 22 • Métro: Filles du Calvaire
Tuesday through Saturday 1pm to 7pm, closed Sunday, Monday
robertleheros.com

STEPPING INTO THE BRIGHT, CHEERY GALLERY OF ROBERT LE HÉROS, ONE CAN INSTANTLY SEE HOW THESE VIBRANT FABRICS AND HOME accessories have become favorites of those who want to inject a bit of color in their lives. The line focuses on flowers, leaf prints, and stripes reminiscent of the south of France, playing across a multitude of items for the *maison*. Little toiletry bags, melamine trays, pillows, tote bags, coated fabric by the meter, as well as a small clothing line for men, women, and children all receive Robert le Heros' fun, lighthearted treatment. New lines are constantly being issued, with names like April Flowers, Under the Plum Tree, and Morning Rain.

Swildens

22, rue du Poitou, 3rd arr.
Telephone: 01 42 71 19 12 • Métro: Saint-Sebastien-Froissart
Monday through Saturday 11am to 2pm, 3pm to 7:30pm, closed Sunday

CREATED BY THE STYLIST WHO STARTED 1 ET 1 FONT 3 ("ONE PLUS ONE MAKES THREE"), THE CHIC FRENCH LINE OF MATERNITY clothes, Swildens is a new label with a laid-back rock 'n' roll look. The black-painted floor and exposed stone of the boutique give it an edgy atmosphere touched with romanticism. Here you'll find blouses with lacy trim, long sweaters and knit jackets in muted colors, leggings and jeans to pair with Pocahontas boots. Check out the line of vintage t-shirts emblazoned with images of the Rolling Stones or Blondie, along with trendy red star scarves, belts with guitar buckles, and thin sterling rings. The impeccable cuts, muted "non-colors," and quality fabrics keep the items from looking too youthful or cheap. The focus is on details and on comfort, for that certain bobo (bourgeois bohemian) look. Model-turned-singer Carla Bruni is a regular.

Titli

19, rue du Pont aux Choux, 3rd arr.
Telephone: 01 44 59 89 17 • Métro: Saint-Sebastien-Froissart
Tuesday through Saturday 2pm to 7pm, closed Sunday, Monday
titli.eu

SITTING BEHIND A WORKBENCH IN A FORMER *CORDONNERIE* (COB-BLER SHOP), EMMANUELLE LIVIO LOOKS LIKE A MODERN-DAY alchemist, turning raw materials into *jolie* jewelry. This mini-boutique contains her collection—works-in-progress hang from hooks on the back wall, while shelves display the current season's line. Livio began her career as a graphic designer and worked in prêt-à-porter. A collector of vintage postcards and mother-of-pearl buttons, she developed a process that combined her two interests by serigraphing vintage imagery onto mother-of-pearl medallions. Some items are sweet and tiny, such as the little mother-of-pearl charms with French sayings ("Bonheur") on them; others are statement pieces like a necklace composed of giant ebony links, but all the pieces are undeniably unique. She produces two collections a year, in a variety of materials such as copper, ebony, silver, semi-precious stones, and handmade silk ribbons. All pieces are made by hand.

4th
Arrondissement

L'Argenterie de Turenne

19, rue de Turenne, 4th arr.
Telephone: 01 42 72 04 00 • Métro: Saint-Paul
Tuesday through Saturday 10:30am to 7pm, closed Sunday

OR MORE THAN THIRTY YEARS, L'ARGENTERIE DE TURENNE HAS OPENED ITS DOORS TO REVEAL A GLEAMING SILVER COLLECTION; the scent of polish wafts through the air. Shelves and cabinets are brimming with silver—silver plate (*métal argenté*) in the front, and

sterling silver (*argent massif*) in the cases at the rear. One of their specialties is hotel silver, which makes this a great place to pick up a fish platter engraved with "Hôtel du Nord" or with the monogram of another grand hotel. There is also a wall lined with a hodge-podge of cutlery—mismatched knives, forks, and spoons—that are sold by the kilo. Why not create several inventive place settings of mixed heritage for the *maison de campagne*? Parisians know that this is the place to come for full sets of vintage silver (Christofle and other major French manufacturers) or to hunt down a missing piece from grandmother's set. Favorite gifts are the sets of the teeny tiny espresso spoons or a set of *très* bourgeois knife rests.

Au Petit Bonheur de Chance

13, rue Saint-Paul, 4th arr.
Telephone: 01 42 74 36 38 • Métro: Saint-Paul
Monday, Thursday and Sunday 11am to 1pm, 2:30pm to 7pm
closed Tuesday, Wednesday

OWNER MARIA-PIA VARNIER HUNTS ALL OVER FRANCE FOR THE COL-
LECTIBLE KITCHEN WARES SHE SELLS IN HER SHOP. HER CROWDED
antique shop is home to
stacks upon stacks of colorful old
café au lait bowls, gadgets, metal
French publicity signs, vintage
stationery from the 1940s, mustard pots, enameled salt boxes,
wooden coffee grinders, and madeleine molds—the types of objects
you find as reproductions at the
upscale gourmet shops stateside.
Here, they're the genuine articles.
Grab up the beautiful hand-
embroidered, monogrammed tea
towels or metal house numbers,
neither of which take up too much
room in a suitcase and can add
that certain French charm to your
maison back home.

Brontibay Paris

6, rue de Sévigné, 4th arr.
Telephone: 01 42 76 90 80 • Métro: Saint-Paul
Monday through Saturday 11am to 8pm, Sunday 1:30pm to 7:30pm
brontibay.fr

THE BRONTIBAY STORY IS THAT OF AUSTRALIAN PENELOPE ROBERT-SON AND FRENCH HUSBAND OLIVIER NAIM, WHO TEAMED UP WITH designer Maud Terseur in 1996 to create this handbag line. The basic white and exposed stone of the shop makes a perfect blank canvas against which to display this trio's creations. The name itself is a combination of two hot surfing spots in Sydney; the bags are definitely infused with sun and fun. Bags are fresh, colorful, and practical without being boring. From the wide range of unstructured bags in bright hues with contrasting handles to the butter-soft leather satchels, the quality is excellent. There is also a range of interesting wallets that tie closed and granny-inspired coin purses. The *fabuleux* satin bow-shaped clutches are lined up on the wall like colorful bonbons, and are equally hard to resist.

Canzi

4, rue Ferdinand Duval, 4th arr.
Telephone: 01 42 78 09 37 • Métro: Saint-Paul
Tuesday through Sunday 10am to 8:30pm, closed Monday
canzi.fr

O
N A SIDE STREET IN THE MARAIS, CANZI STOCKS THE BEST IN EURO-
PEAN ORGANIC (*BIO*) PERFUMES AND COSMETICS ALONG WITH ITS
own brand. The house brand includes products that can be created
sur mesure using only natural, organic ingredients, along with ready-made
potions such as the noteworthy *Lotion Précieuse à la Rose*. Here, the offerings include everything from massage oils to toothpaste to perfumes, along
with a range of essential oils. Inspired by the needs of different skin types,
owner Stéphane Mottay also runs a workshop/atelier where clients learn
to mix their own potions such as exfoliants and masks. At the Monday
evening workshops, customers are taught how to make natural formulas,
using fresh, organic ingredients with the addition of fragrances and active
ingredients that work best for each individual.

Carabosse

11, rue de Sévigné, 4th arr.
Telephone: 01 44 61 05 98 • Métro: Saint-Paul
Tuesday through Saturday 11am to 7pm, Sunday 3pm to 7pm
carabosse.eu

NAMED AFTER A WICKED WITCH CHARACTER IN A FRENCH CHILDREN'S STORY, THIS ORIGINAL CHILDREN'S SHOP IN THE MARAIS has a slightly sinister side, but all in good fun. A bit like Petit Bateau, but with an urban edge, Carabosse knitwear uses bold stripes and solids, matching black, putty, and gray with brights—a refreshing change from the *rose pale/bleu ciel* collections offered in many other Parisian shops. The funky stripes often make an appearance in several colors on one garment. Visible stitching is another distinctive feature. The simple shapes —A-line dresses, wrap tops, t-shirts, baggy pants—are all made in France, for sizes 0 to 10. Much of the collection is unisex. Accessories such as booties, hats, and scarves round out the well-made collection.

Entrée des Fournisseurs

8, rue Francs Bourgeois [in courtyard], 4th arr.
Telephone: 01 48 87 58 98 • Métro: Saint-Paul
Monday 2pm to 7pm, Tuesday through Saturday
10:30am to 7pm, closed Sunday
entreedesfournisseurs.com

YOU HAVE TO BE REALLY LOOKING TO FIND ENTRÉE DES FOURNIS-
SEURS, WHICH IS TUCKED AWAY IN AN IVY-COVERED COURTYARD
(indeed, the name means "Supplier's Entrance"). The light-filled
boutique is filled with fabulous notions, making any one with a creative
urge long to get home to whip something up using the supplies provided
by this shop. Iron racks and old wooden counters hold hundreds of bolts of
ribbons, embroidery and knitting supplies,
fabric and sequined flowers, and French
labels (*Je t'aime*) to sew inside handmade
items. Customers come by to get new buttons to give a facelift to an old jacket or
to pick up one of the cute knitting kits to
make the perfect layette gift. While the
shop specializes in notions, a nice selection
of Liberty-print fabrics and thick wool felt
is sold by the meter, both of which can be
used in the Citronille patterns (also sold
here) to make dresses, tunics, or tote bags.

K. Jacques

16, rue Pavée, 4th arr.
Telephone: 01 40 27 03 57 • Métro: Staint-Paul
Monday through Saturday 10:30am to 7pm, Sunday 2pm to 7pm
lestropeziennes.com

TARTED BY MONSIEUR AND MADAME JACQUES IN 1933, ST. TROPEZ'S MOST FAMOUS SANDAL MAKER STILL REIGNS SUPREME FOR ITS simple, timeless styles. The tiny boutique in St. Tropez started with custom sandals for celebrity clients vacationing in the ritzy beach town; the family-owned business still caters to the same crowd, as well as mere mortals. One of its most famous styles, the Spartiate, first introduced decades ago, was back at the height of fashion summer 2007 and remains a classic addition to every wardrobe. In the miniscule, crowded Paris show-room, check out other styles for women, men, and children—you'll find styles ranging from a super-simple thong to a gladiator that wraps up the calf. All the sandals develop a patina over time and are the kind of thing that you keep for years; they have a timeless look, perfect with jeans and a white t-shirt. And if the exact model you want isn't in stock, a *sur mesure* service is available, with at least fifty different models to choose from and more than 100 finishes in a variety of materials (python, metallic, patent leather, etc.). Delivery times range from one to three weeks depending on the time of year. The brand has also created sandals for some of the most prestigious fashion houses, including Lagerfeld, Kenzo, and Missoni.

Lobato

6, rue Malher, 4th arr.
Telephone: 01 48 87 68 14 • Métro: Saint-Paul
Monday through Saturday 11am to 7pm, closed Sunday
lobato-paris.com

WALK BEHIND THIS SHEER-CURTAINED DOOR IN THE MARAIS TO A MODERN, WHITE *BOÎTE DE BIJOUX*—ONLY IN THIS JEWEL BOX, the gems are shoes. Miguel Lobato is on hand to offer you the best in European shoes and bags from the likes of Charlott Vasberg, Mosse, and Vincent du Sartel, along with bigger names such as Michel Vivien. His shop is small and intimate, and the collection is carefully curated. Lobato himself tests each pair to insure that the heel isn't too high and that the fit is comfortable for everyday life in Paris. His specialty is city chic—finding shoes that are not only gorgeous enough for the most posh Parisienne but able to withstand cobblestone streets and Métro steps. Models and other fashion world types stop by regularly to view Lobato's collection of the best of the best *chaussures* and bags.

Lotta & Djossou

11, rue Ferdinand Duval, 4th arr.
Telephone: 01 42 71 79 61 • Métro: Saint-Paul
Tuesday through Sunday noon to 7pm
lottadjossou.com

DESIGNERS LOTTA ANDERSSON AND CLEMENT DJOSSOU—SHE A DESIGNER, HE A SILVERSMITH—HAD SHOPS IN TOKYO AND Sweden before moving to Paris in 2002. Their boutique in the Marais, a funky, romantic mix of antique furniture and exposed stone walls, houses their varied collections of jewelry. All sorts of materials go into their work—Swarovski crystals, chunky pieces of turquoise, semi-precious stones and natural pearls, set in silver or brass. Motifs might include romantic flowers, autumnal leaves, or an Asian theme. They call their style "ethnic chic," inspired by travels worldwide. The collection is sophisticated but sweet, and affordably priced.

Nicole Lehmann

19, rue de Turenne, 4th arr.
Telephone: 01 42 77 57 21 • Métro: Saint-Paul
Tuesday through Saturday 11am to 7pm, Sunday
2pm to 7pm, closed Monday
nlparis.com

NICOLE LEHMANN'S NEW SHOP JUST A BLOCK AWAY FROM THE PLACE DES VOSGES IS SMALL BUT ELEGANT, THE PERFECT SETTING for showing off her luxurious purses. Each of her bags is entirely handmade, with attention to fine details, in high-quality leathers and skins with metal accents. The bags come in three basic styles: the *cabas* (tote), the *pochette* (clutch), and the *besace* (messenger). Each comes with either long or short straps and in different finishes (grained or smooth leather, suede, alligator, ostrich). Some have unique details such as a long chain strap that can be removed and worn as a necklace; another style has a slim leather closure strap that is interchangeable with straps of other colors, and any of the straps can be worn as a bracelet. A small line of jewelry, cuff links, and belts rounds out the collection.

Sandro

50, rue Vielle du Temple, 4th arr.
Telephone: 01 44 59 69 23 • Métro: Hôtel de Ville
Sunday through Monday 1pm to 7pm
Tuesday through Saturday 10am to 7pm
sandro-paris.com

IT'S A RAGS-TO-RICHES STORY: IN 1980, EVELYNE CHÉTRITE STARTED THIS CLOTHING BRAND WITH HUSBAND DIDIER IN THE WHOLESALE district of Paris, the Sentier, where prices are cheap and where small designers don't follow the traditional *prêt* seasons, but are constantly coming out with new garments throughout the year. About five years ago, they left the semi-seedy neighborhood for a nicer area and took their brand to a higher level, adopting traditional *prêt* seasons and price points. The brand quickly rose in popularity among the young trendy set and has become a staple in many wardrobes. The fine materials and romantic, graceful styles are modern and just trendy enough. The line includes soft cashmere *pulls*, loads of little dresses, and well-cut jackets. The light-filled Sandro boutiques, such as this corner shop in the Marais, are popping up all over the city, but the brand is not yet available stateside. Stop by to pick up sweet, well-tailored chic looks that blend in easily to your *garde-robe*.

Sentou

❧

29, rue François Miron, 4th arr.
Telephone: 01 42 78 50 60 • Métro: Saint-Paul, Hôtel de Ville
Monday 2pm to 7pm, Tuesday through Saturday
10am to 7pm, closed Sunday
sentou.fr

IN 1947, ROBERT SENTOU STARTED MANUFACTURING FURNITURE BY MAJOR DESIGNERS IN HIS OWN FACTORY. IN THE 1970S, HE SET UP shop in Paris to showcase his work, and in 1991 turned the reigns of the shop over to Pierre Romanet. Since then, the *magasin* has become synonymous with modern design and fresh, contemporary decor for the home. Romanet has grouped together the creations of modern designers in two shops in the Marais and another one in Saint-Germain. On the border of the Marais, the light-filled rue Miron shop focuses on furniture and lighting from brands like Verner Panton, Jean Prouvé, Charles and Rae Eames and others. Just down the block, the corner shop on rue du Pont Louis Philippe focuses on dishes, linens, vases, decorative objects, mirrors, and gift items. Here you'll find creations such as the famous test-tube-inspired Avril vase by Tsé & Tsé, 100drine's fun, kid-like metal storage boxes, mod clocks by George Nelson, and colorful ceramic tableware by Brigitte de Bazelaire.

Skeen+

21, rue des Archives, 4th arr.
Telephone: 01 42 76 04 07 • Métro: Hôtel de Ville, Rambuteau
Monday, Wednesday through Saturday 11am to 7pm,
Sunday noon to 7pm, closed Tuesday
skeen.fr

FOR THE LATEST IN MEN'S SKINCARE FOR THE *HOMME* IN YOUR LIFE, CHECK OUT SKEEN+, BASED ON FORMULAS DESIGNED TO be efficient, hypoallergenic, and highly effective. Any man will be happy to open a medicine cabinet to find the range of grooming products with distinctive matte black-and-white bottles with stylish lab-like labels. The products contain no artificial fragrances or coloring but do include active ingredients like retinol and Vitamin C and are made specifically for men—their skin, thicker and oilier than women's, needs different products. The products have simple, straightforward names (Concentrated Anti-Wrinkle Formula, Soothing Fluid Balm, Daily Rich Shampoo) and color-coded bottles for easy identification. The Diagnosis Lab helps clients choose the appropriate products.

Xuan-Thu Nguyen

1, rue Ferdinand Duval, 4th arr.
Telephone: 01 42 77 08 60 • Métro: Saint-Paul
Tuesday through Sunday 11am to 7pm
xuan-thunguyen.com

TUCKED AWAY ON ONE OF THE QUIETER STREETS IN THE MARAIS, XUAN-THU NGUYEN'S BOUTIQUE IS A CALM, DELICATE SPACE FILLED with her one-of-a-kind fashion creations. Vietnam-born, Netherlands-raised Nguyen opened her shop in 2004 to showcase her unique style—modern, geometrical shapes with delicate details and natural fabrics. She emphasizes fine craftsmanship and strives to have the finished garments free of visible stitches and full of hidden details. The interesting cuts feature Nguyen's trademark flat waist bands, reversed embroidery, and perfect side finishes. The result is extravagant and simple at the same time. You may find a shirt with an ultra-high neck or a dress with an extra pouffy sleeve: the look is original and timelessly elegant. Nguyen plays with volumes in her accessories as well, as in the uber-chunky beaded necklaces or accordion-pleated scarves.

Yukiko

97, rue Vielle du Temple, 4th arr.
Telephone: 01 42 71 13 41 • Métro: Saint-Sebastien-Froissart
Monday through Saturday 11am to 7pm, closed Sunday
yukiko-paris.com

OPEN SINCE 2002 IN THE HIP HAUTE MARAIS NEIGHBORHOOD, YUKIKO IS A LADUREE-GREEN JEWEL BOX OF A BOUTIQUE, with vintage treasures and Yukiko's own accessories line. You'll find rare 1960s-1980s Hermès, 1970s-1990s Chanel, 1970s Dior, and 1970s

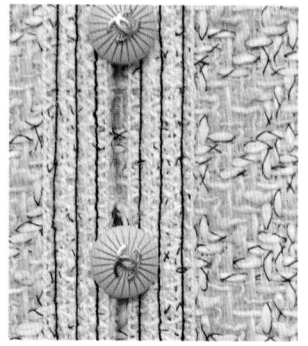

Gucci pieces that she has been collecting for over a decade. She also stocks her own collection, started three years ago, which includes mink fur pieces (stoles, pink embroidered vests), silky cocktail dresses, and girly jewelry such as charm bracelets. With clients from all over the world (Kate Moss and Penelope Cruz have both stopped in) and two more shops in Japan, Yukiko's mini boutique is a *tresor* you don't want to miss.

5th
Arrondissement

Côté Bastide

4, rue de Poissy, 5th arr.
Telephone: 01 56 24 01 21 • Métro: Maubert-Mutualité
Monday through Saturday 10:30am to 7pm
cotebastide.com

CÔTÉ BASTIDE'S LUXURIOUS, FLORAL TOILETRY PRODUCTS AND HOME DECOR ITEMS EMBODY THE PROVENÇAL COUNTRYSIDE. THE shop's overall look is that of whitewashed walls, oiled wooden floors, terracotta tiles and flowing white linens, with a clean, pleasant fragrance wafting throughout. Perfumes for personal use and for the home (in fresh scents like fig tree, vetiver, and vineyard peach), bath salts, triple-milled embossed soaps, creams and lotions are for sale in gorgeous apothecary bottles and jars reminiscent of times past. The boutique stocks all sorts of things for the home as well—bed and bath linens, glassware and ceramics, candleholders and lamps—to complete the elegant look.

6th
Arrondissement

Adelline

~~~

54, rue Jacob, 6th arr.
Telephone: 01 47 03 07 18 • Métro: Saint-Germain-des-Près, Rue du Bac
Monday through Saturday 10:30am to 7pm, closed Sunday

ON A STREET IN THE MIDST OF SAINT-GERMAIN ART GALLERIES, JEWELRY CREATOR ADELINE ROUSSEL'S BIJOUX SHINE LIKE LITTLE *OBJETS D'ART*. The dark brown lacquered exterior gives way to a golden, elegant interior filled with lovely gems. Browse the tall cases filled with her creations or sit down in the charming sitting area to leisurely peruse the collection. Easy-to-wear items that are modern and elegant are her specialty and the sensibility can be found in bracelets, necklaces, and dangly earrings—a lovely lacy gold *tuile* cuff, for instance, or pretty matte gold earrings dangling with a row of smoky topaz. Roussel finds her gems in India, and works with her craftsmen there to make semiprecious stones and twenty-two-karat gold look effortlessly chic. Unpolished gold, interesting cuts, and a delicate touch make this a stop for anyone looking for a fresh approach to fine jewelry.

Alexandra Sojfer

218, boulevard Saint-Germain, 6th arr.
Telephone: 01 42 22 17 02 • Métro: Saint-Germain-des-Près
Monday through Saturday 9:30am to 7pm, closed Sunday
alexandrasojfer.fr

T HE FADED METAL UMBRELLAS THAT DECORATE THE EXTERIOR OF THIS BOUTIQUE HAVE SEEN THEIR SHARE OF WEATHER. ON A BLOCK of modern furniture showrooms, this shop is a glimpse of Paris' past. Alexandra Sojfer, the *patronne* of this venerable establishment, trained as an artisan umbrella maker in the family business started by her grandfather and then passed on to her through her mother. In 2002, her family's business merged with that of the famed Madeleine Gely (founded in 1834), and their names are now side by side on the façade. The tiny shop

recently doubled in size (unfortunately, the atelier moved off-site), and sells umbrellas, canes, and parasols with details such as fabric with delicate cut-outs or dangling beads; or for men, elegant stripes. With hand-carved handles, special water-resistant fabric and contrasting linings, these are umbrellas that are cherished for a lifetime. The amusing, seasonal window displays remind us not to take this shop too seriously, as does the giant parasol that creates part of the ceiling inside.

Assouline

35, rue Bonaparte, 6th arr.
Telephone: 01 43 29 23 20 • Métro: Saint-Germain-des-Prés
Monday noon to 7pm, Tuesday through Saturday
10:30am to 7:30pm, closed Sunday
assoulinefrance.com

AS YOU MOVE FROM THE SMARTLY PACKAGED LIMITED EDITIONS TO THE NEATLY ARRANGED WALL OF BOOKS IN THE BACK, IT becomes clear that there are no dusty old tomes here—Assouline is all about luxury, and the shiny volumes on culture, art, and fashion attest to that. The brand, started in 1994, publishes sophisticated, sleek books. Originally sold only in other outlets, the publishing house opened their first flagship shop in Saint-Germain (historically, Paris' intellectual center) in 2006. Now the company counts over 600 titles, in French and in English, as well as *luxe* objects for the home and library. Part of the charm of this light-filled yet cozy space is the array of unexpected items—from the small vintage-look suitcase filled with travel books on the world's best cities, the special black-quilted slipcase housing a volume on Chanel, a book-filled limited-edition Goyard trunk, or scented candles and monogrammed ostrich eggs to decorate your home *bibliothèque*.

Blanc d'Ivoire

4, rue Jacob, 6th arr.
Telephone: 01 46 33 34 29 • Métro: Saint-Germain-des-Prés
Monday 12:30pm to 7pm, Tuesday through Saturday
10:30am to 7pm, closed Sunday
blancdivoire.com

FOR A MODERN TAKE ON THE FRENCH COUNTRY LOOK, STEP INTO THIS WELCOMING BOUTIQUE. MOST OF THE SHOP IS DECORATED in soothing neutrals—grays and whites dominate. The overall look is that of a very tasteful *maison de campagne*, with a Provençal-meets-Gustavian esthetic, romantic yet sophisticated. Furniture is copied from antique models, complete with patinas and well-worn finishes. If you aren't planning on taking home the furniture, check out the smalls, all done in a somewhat modern, not cloyingly sweet style—gorgeous matel-assé quilts, pillows, glassware, lamps, and silver accessories for the table. A tiny back room offers table linens and curtains in white and beige.

Bois de Rose

30, rue Dauphine, 6th arr.
Telephone: 01 40 46 04 24 • Métro: Mabillon
Monday through Saturday 10:30am to 7pm, closed Sunday
boisderose.fr

FOR A *JEUNE FILLE FRANÇAISE*, THERE IS NOTHING MORE CLASSIC THAN A LITTLE SMOCKED DRESS. THIS SHOP CARRIES A LARGE range at very reasonable prices, seemingly in every color imaginable, up to size 14. The smocking can be simple or in whimsical designs such as sailboats or strawberries. To make sure dolly is also à *la mode*, there are miniature frocks to match the ones for little girls. Headbands, barrettes, and basket purses trimmed to match are also offered. Bois de Rose specializes in children's outfits for weddings, baptisms, and other special occasions—long silk or cotton dresses with matching jackets and knickers with suspenders for boys (also up to size 14). Classic baby gifts include embroidered bibs and sleep sacks, and if you don't find exactly what you are looking for, special orders are available and take about two months.

Cire Trudon

78, rue de Seine, 6th arr.
Telephone: 01 43 26 46 50 • Métro: Mabillon
Monday through Saturday 10am to 1pm, 2:15pm to 7pm, closed Sunday
cirier.com

HIS COMPANY, FOUNDED IN 1643 (THE OLDEST CANDLE MANUFAC-
TURER IN THE WORLD) AND PREVIOUSLY CALLED CIR, WAS A ROYAL
purveyor of candles for Louis XVII and continues to provide candles for
churches, palaces, and haute couture houses throughout France. The boutique
has recently had a *très belle* makeover. The "relooking," by artistic director
Ramdane Touhami, moved the kitschy line of fantasy candles (in the shape of

French cheeses, birds, dogs, and the
Eiffel Tower) upstairs, making way for
a stylish new space. The main part of
the boutique is now lined with antique-
looking British wallpaper and dramatic
black shelves, which set off the thirty-
six colors of tapers displayed along one
wall. A lush line of scented white and
off-white pillars adorned with cameos
and wax candle statues of Napoleon
and Marie Antoinette are part of the
new collection, as is a custom service
offering candles with personalized text,
colors, or photos. Scented candles, in

hand-blown glass containers and with gold engraved labels, come in fragrances such as the Roi Soleil (The Sun King), Dada, Odeur de Lune (Moon Scent), La Marquise, and more. A special *cave*, unchanged since the eighteenth century and lit only with candles, displays additional treasures. The candles are all natural, made with vegetable waxes, and contain no paraffin or petrochemicals, which allows them to hold fragrance longer and results in a clean, long-burning candle.

La Compagnie de Provence Marseille

5, rue Brea, 6th arr.
Telephone: 01 43 26 39 53 • Métro: Vavin
Tuesday through Saturday 10:30am to 2pm, 3pm to 7:30pm
closed Sunday, Monday
lcdpmarseille.com

L A COMPAGNIE DE PROVENCE MARSEILLE WAS STARTED IN 1990 BY A PAIR OF MARSEILLAISE FRIENDS WHO WANTED TO TAKE THE FAMOUS cube-shaped *savon de Marseille* to a different level. The line's brown paper packaging tied with string was an instant hit, and the pair moved on to reinventing and reinterpreting other bathroom basics. The results are fresh, yet classic, appealing to those who like modern design as well as those who long for the traditional article. Graphic style—such as the shape of their pump bottle—and innovative, streamlined packaging have made the products a must-have for many stylish *salle de bains*. Walking into the boutique, one is enveloped by the clean scent of soap. The simple layout of the shop includes zinc-topped wooden tables and open shelving housing rows of products, including the original blocks of soap, as well as lotions, travel sizes, and towels and bath mats to complement the collection. Check out the über-chic, all-black bottle of Ylang Noir Pur Soap or the Verbena Linen Water.

Comptoir des Cotonniers

30, rue de Buci, 6th arr.
Telephone: 01 43 54 56 73 • Métro: Mabillon
Monday 11am to 7pm, Tuesday through Saturday
10am to 7pm, closed Sunday
comptoirdescotonniers.com

THIS EASY-TO-WEAR FRENCH LINE HAS BECOME A STAPLE OF MANY A FRENCH WOMAN'S WARDROBE SINCE ITS DEBUT IN 1995. THE CLASSIC, well-cut pieces are just trendy enough, yet wearable for a few years forward without looking *passé*. The company's famous marketing campaign features real mothers and daughters modeling the clothing—a reflection of the real world in which teens as well as their *mères* snap up the collections. The clothing is simple, well made, and slightly preppy with just the right amount of detail. The color palette is usually basic, with grays, taupes, and blacks anchoring most of the collection, although each season one color (such as lemon yellow or cherry red) makes an appearance in a sweet print on blouses and trench coat linings. Lots of little jackets, pants in different styles, swingy dresses, and layered sweaters are included in the range. A few bags (large leather totes, cute canvas clutches) and a few pairs of shoes (such as a special edition Nike or rubber rain boot) round out the collection.

JC Martinez

21, rue Saint-Sulpice, 6th arr.
Telephone: 01 43 26 34 53 • Métro: Saint-Sulpice
Monday through Saturday 10:30am to 12.20pm
2pm to 6:30pm, closed Sunday
jean-claude-martinez.fr

IF YOU DON'T WANT TO MAKE THE TREK TO THE PUCES, GO TO JC MARTINEZ TO FIND AN OLD ENGRAVED PRINT OR MAP. THE WELCOMING bright red façade showcases a changing collection of gorgeous maps and prints, lovingly arranged. The window displays also exhibit vintage posters and small framed prints according to seasonal themes. The helpful staff will help you discover the large well-organized and well-priced collection of prints from the sixteenth century onward, neatly filed away in huge folders by subject. Whether you are looking for pigeons or perfumes, eyeglasses or elephants, you'll find it here—the subject list goes on and on. The shop stocks a selection of collector's books as well.

Karine Dupont

16, rue du Cherche-Midi, 6th arr.
Telephone: 01 42 84 06 30 • Métro: Sevres-Babylone
Monday through Saturday 11am to 2:30pm
3:30pm to 7pm, closed Sunday
karinedupont.com

LIVELY, PRACTICAL, AND FUN, KARINE DUPONT IS A LOT LIKE THE BAGS SHE CREATES. THIRTY-SOMETHING DUPONT WENT TO FASHION school and started her career designing for French jewelry lines Agatha and Reminiscence, before turning to bags. The K3, one of her first creations, is still a best seller years later; it is made up of three pockets in the same tones, that can be interchanged or removed as needed. Her cheery turquoise Saint-Germain boutique opened in 2000, stocking the basic collection along with new models that change with the season. Dupont now offers colorful totes with long or short handles, the K3 in leather or fabric, in tiny sizes up to the large weekend styles. Great leather satchels are also on offer. Much of the collection is made in limited numbers, depending on the amount of high-quality leather that can be found. Karine's motto, *"Osez et suivez vos envies"* (Dare to follow your dreams) is inscribed on one wall of the boutique; her bright, fun bags might make you want to grab one and do just that.

Marie Papier

26, rue Vavin, 6th arr.
Telephone: 01 43 26 46 44 • Métro: Vavin
Monday 2pm to 7pm, Tuesday through Saturday
10am to 7pm, closed Sunday
mariepapier.fr

O N A QUIET STREET FILLED WITH OTHER QUAINT NEIGHBORHOOD BOUTIQUES, MARIE PAPIER'S BLACK STOREFRONT SETS A FRAME for the intense jewel tones of the paper goods inside. The concept of a paper boutique was a new one in 1977 when Marie-Paule Orluc, a former art director, after working with Elizabeth Arden and *Marie Claire*, opened the shop. Orluc's sophisticated fashion sensibilities are apparent in her eye for color—papers range from a refined pearl gray to an eye-popping turquoise. Cards and envelopes are available in every format, in

hundreds of hues, all available for engraving. All of the gorgeously simple products are of excellent quality, and range from photo albums and journals to stationery, as well as all the notions and desk accessories that go with them. The little packs of colored *cartes de visite*, tied with ribbon, make great gifts, as do the traditional-French *livres d'or* (guest books).

Marie Puce

16, rue Bréa, 6th arr.
Telephone: 01 43 54 43 32 • Métro: Vavin
Monday 1:30pm to 7pm, Tuesday through Saturday
11am to 7pm, closed Sunday
mariepuce.com

*I*F LIBERTY PRINTS ARE YOUR STYLE, LOOK NO FURTHER THAN THE MARIE PUCE BOUTIQUE. THIS SMALL, CHARMING SHOP, WITH ITS pint-sized racks, offers simple, high quality, refined looks for tots and bigger kids, sizes up to 12 for some models and up to 18 for others (svelte *mamans* can match their daughters). For *les filles*, there are tunic blouses in Liberty prints as well as the corduroy shorts and tights that little

French girls wear with them. You'll also find graceful A-line dresses and simple empire-waist jumpers in solid colors to wear with Liberty blouses or coordinating t-shirts. For *les garçons*, there are little woolen pants for winter and linen Bermuda shorts to pair with t-shirts or collarless cotton shirts in summer. The baby line includes tiny cotton bloomers and rompers and matching pants and tees. The color palette is refined and muted; no neon brights here. Created in 2003 by Camille Rey and Anne Thin, sisters with six children between them, this shop is a fave of the refined and preppy Luxembourg garden crowd. Other items to look for are the personalized stenciled toiletry bags, cute nighties, and other children's accessories by Lin & cie ("Linen and Company"), and a line of simple, sweet children's jewelry.

Mis en Demeure

27, rue du Cherche-Midi, 6th arr.
Telephone: 01 45 48 83 79 • Métro: Sevres-Babylone
Monday 1pm to 7pm, Tuesday through Saturday
10am to 7pm, closed Sunday
misendemeure.com

FOR AN INSTANT LESSON IN DISTINCTIVELY FRENCH DECORATING, HEAD TO MIS EN DEMEURE'S INSPIRED BOUTIQUE, SET IN A dramatic turn-of-the-century apartment. The style is a mix of classic French looks (gilded mirrors, modern velvet sofas, handsome armchairs) along with a few antiques such as statues, architectural pieces, and giant old clock faces. This is the flea market, only better—updated, redone, cleaned up and very livable. Check out the lovely line of table and bed linens, in a range of rich colors, the silver and shell table accessories, small framed prints, and gorgeous lamps. Even if you aren't shopping for home decor at all, strolling around this shop will please your voyeuristic side, making you feel as if you are peeking into a sophisticated Parisian flat.

N. Villaret

20, rue de Cherche-Midi, 6th arr.
Telephone: 01 45 44 02 50 • Métro: Sevres-Babylone
Monday 2:30pm to 7pm, Tuesday through Saturday 10:30am to 1:30pm,
2:30pm to 7pm, closed Sunday
n-villaret.com

IN THIS QUAINT SHABBY-CHIC SHOP IN SAINT-GERMAIN, YOU'LL FIND NICOLE VILLARET'S TAKE ON TRADITIONAL FRENCH COUNTRY linens: quilts, sheets, shams, and tablecloths in flowered prints, toile de Jouy, stripes, and solids, all in lovely muted tones in linen or cotton pique. Almost all are reversible and can be mixed and matched for a cozy, homey look. Large, quilted throws can be used in the home in a variety of ways—as a bedcover, a tablecloth, or a throw. Villaret, who started her career as a stylist, created her demure line of linens in 1991 to capture the distinctive French *art de vivre*. The linens respect tradition, and look to the past; they're tasteful, elegant, and simply French. You'll also find fabric-covered boxes, aprons, and lampshades.

Nadine Delepine

14, rue Princesse, 6th arr.
Telephone: 01 40 51 81 10 • Métro: Mabillon
Monday through Saturday 11am to 7pm, closed Sunday
nadinedelepine.com

IN HER SHOP ON A SECLUDED STREET IN SAINT-GERMAIN, NADINE DELEPINE CREATES JEWELRY, HATS, BAGS, AND A SMALL CLOTHING line. Her atelier, where she makes her romantic, girly bijoux, is visible in the rear of the shop. Using typically feminine motifs (flowers, butterflies, and birds) and materials (lace and pearls), her pieces are a touch Victorian while remaining *moderne*. Her mixed-material designs also grace hairpins, coin purses, pillboxes, and headbands. Purses and hats are offered in seasonal materials—Liberty cottons in warm months and wool tweeds in cool. If you don't find the color or design that you are looking for, Delepine will create something for you. She also specializes in *sur mesure* items for weddings and other events.

Les Olivades

1, rue de Tournon, 6th arr.
Telephone: 01 43 54 14 54 • Métro: Mabillon, Saint-Sulpice
Monday through Saturday 10am to 1pm, 2pm to 7pm, closed Sunday
lesolivades.fr

LES OLIVADES SPECIALIZES IN PRINTED PROVENÇAL FABRICS AND HOMEWARES. THE SHOP IN SAINT-GERMAIN OFFERS A WIDE RANGE OF products, such as fabric by the meter, acrylic-coated *tissus enduits* (water-resistant fabric), ceramics, lamps, accessories, throws, trays, and pillows, all in bright Provençal colors and patterns. Elaborate motifs such as stripes, paisleys, florals, and toiles, as well as fruit and bee themes, are standard, but the line offers some uncomplicated prints that are more modern and graphic. Les Olivades also produces a line of clothing (sold at the shop down the street, at 95, rue de Seine), which includes women's scarves, simple pants, tunics, and bags made out of the famous prints, as well as paisley shirts and ties for men.

Oona L'Ourse

72, rue Madame, 6th arr.
Telephone: 01 42 84 11 94 • Métro: Saint-Placide
Monday 2:30pm to 6:30pm, Tuesday through Saturday
11am to 6:30pm, closed Sunday
oonalourse.com

IN THIS SHOP JUST A BLOCK AWAY FROM THE LOVELY JARDIN DU LUXEMBOURG, JANE FICHARD DISPLAYS CHILDREN'S CLOTHING THAT still looks like children's clothing. No flashy colors or mini-me designs here, but the classic, well-made children's wear beloved by the French: flowered Liberty print bloomers, little white blouses, and pleated sleeveless dresses for girls, v-neck sweaters and tweed blazers for boys. While the materials are classic, the cuts are updated for today's fashion, with pants cut slimmer to follow recent trends, or skirts filled with hidden pockets to hide one's treasures. Fichard, who is French but with an English background, combines Gallic allure and British sensibility in her clothing for the under-ten crowd. The clothing is an updated version of a timeless, elegant French look, with a nod to the past.

Pierre Frey Accessories

1-2, rue de Furstenberg, 6th arr.
Telephone: 01 46 33 73 00 • Métro: Saint-Germain-des-Prés, Odéon
Monday through Saturday 10am to 7pm, closed Sunday
Pierrefrey.com

STARTED BY PIERRE FREY IN 1935 AND MANAGED BY SON PATRICK SINCE 1976, PIERRE FREY IS *THE* NAME FOR LUXURY FRENCH WOVEN and printed fabrics. The showrooms in Paris stock more than 3500 fabrics, sought out by decorators throughout the world. This small shop, near the delightful Place Furstenberg, houses Pierre Frey's household accessories line: throws, bags, china accents, trays and other accents that complement the fabrics or can stand alone. Nearby, you'll find the brand's fabric and furniture showrooms, which showcase their eponymous line as well as other house brands Braquenié (specializing in eighteenth- and nineteenth-century prints and haute couture rugs), Fadini Borghi (silk fabric), Boussac (known for its jacquards and hotel collections), and Romanex (cotton prints).

Sabbia Rosa

73, rue des Saints-Pères, 6th arr.
Telephone: 01 45 48 88 37 • Métro: Saint-Germain-des-Prés
Monday through Saturday 10am to 7pm, closed Sunday

FOR MORE THAN THIRTY YEARS IN THE SAME BOUTIQUE, THE QUALIFIED *VENDEUSES* AT SABBIA ROSA HAVE BEEN OFFERING advice on silk, satin, and lace. The quaint boudoir-like shop, with soft lighting and a *très* feminine ambiance, stocks luxurious lingerie in natural fabrics like linen, silk, and cotton, with details like reknowned Calais lace. Silk nightgowns, slips, and camisoles are hung hundreds to a hanger, the large range of colors making it seem impossible to choose. Fear not, however, as one of the lovely saleswomen, who are often wearing the shop's items (maybe a chartreuse camisole peeking out from under a cashmere cardigan), will help you find what you need. After a detailed conversation as to preferred style, and considering skin tone and hair color, she will pull out an assortment of lace and satin bras and panties from the little drawers, and she will almost always be spot-on in her choices. Madonna and Catherine Deneuve are clients. A *sur mesure* service is available as well.

Sabre

4, rue des Quatre Vents, 6th arr.
Telephone: 01 44 07 37 64 • Métro: Odéon
Monday through Saturday 10am to 1pm
1:30pm to 7:15pm, closed Sunday
sabre.fr

THE KITCHEN LINE SABRE IS DISTINGUISHED BY COLORFUL, FUN TABLEWARE FOR EVERY DAY. THE LINE STARTED WITH PLASTIC-HANDLED cutlery, available in a range of upbeat patterns and solids—from floral prints to ginghams to toiles, stripes, and houndstooth, along with simple faux horn, ivory, and bamboo. A line of ceramic tableware complements the original flatware line. You'll find polka-dot espresso cups with cheery flowered saucers, and other must-have accessories such as knife rests, napkin rings, serving trays, and simple metal tins for showing off the colorful cutlery. The look is fun, imaginative, and contemporary, and not at all fussy like many other French table lines. Nothing is sold as a set—all are individual pieces—so that clients may mix and match according to their whimsy.

Servane Gaxotte

55, rue des Sainta-Pères, 6th arr.
Telephone: 01 42 84 39 93 • Métro: Rue du Bac
Monday through Saturday 11am to 7pm, closed Sunday

A JEWELRY-BOX SIZED BOUTIQUE IS THE PERFECT PLACE FOR SHOWING OFF SERVANE GAXOTTE'S SWEET AND CHARMING line of bijoux. One wall of the shop displays a delicate art piece of bronze nails in a fantastic design that functions as three-dimensional wallpaper and holds her necklaces at the same time. Gaxotte's delicate and refined jewelry is just a tad rock 'n' roll, taking sweetness down a notch and making it the perfect thing to spice up your collection. Famous for her *poupée* (babydoll) necklaces—tiny articulated dolls with different outfits and expressions—Gaxotte also produces a line of fun, fantasy jewelry that mixes metal, fabric, sequins, and charms. Large bronze linked necklaces or leather cords hold *amusant* pendants such as mini-mice, feathers, or small purses engraved with "*super maman*" and "*je t'aime.*" The look is unique and charming, much like the *créatrice* herself.

Tara Jarmon

75, rue des Saints-Pères, 6th arr.
Telephone: 01 45 44 36 14 • Métro: Saint-Sulpice, Sevres-Babylone
Monday through Saturday 11am to 7pm, closed Sunday
tarajarmon.com

TARA JARMON'S IMAGINATIVE COLLECTIONS ARE SLIGHTLY RETRO, BUT ALWAYS ELEGANT. DETAILS SUCH AS FLOWERS, OVERSIZED BUTTONS, and bows play into the styles, which are sexy but never provocative. The materials—cotton, satin, silk, velvet, brocade—and vintage-modern styles stay current for years. The cuts are streamlined and ladylike, flattering to slim figures as well as curvy ones; fashionable, but never fashion-victim. The line is as popular with the teen crowd (swingy mini-dresses) as it is for their *mères*, who snap up the silk blouses and timeless wool coats. Jarmon's line is offered throughout Europe and Asia, but there are no stateside shops yet (although she once designed a line for Target).

Vannina Vesperini

4, rue de Tournon, 6th arr.
Telephone: **01 56 24 32 72** • Métro: **Odéon**
Call for hours
vesperini.fr

AFTER ATTENDING FASHION SCHOOL AND WORKING WITH SOME WELL-KNOWN LINGERIE CREATORS, CORSICAN-BORN Vesperini started her own line in 1996 to create lingerie that could be worn hidden or not. Her new Saint-Germain shop, right next to luxe children's brand Bonpoint, is elegant and intimate, with gold leaf walls and a touch of the Italian Renaissance in the decor. Sexy and glamorous, her looks can be worn in the daytime as well as at night, depending on how you play it. The first floor displays her collection of bras, panties, bustiers, nightgowns, shorties, and other little tops in Calais lace, Lyonnaise silk, cashmere, cotton, or Lycra, with a focus on quality materials that give a nice line to the figure. Colors range from the palest to the brightest, along with stripes and dots—this is lingerie that is so gorgeous it really is a shame to hide it. The second floor has a private salon for custom items, made by Ms. Vesperini herself.

7th
Arrondissement

Carine Gilson

18, rue de Grenelle, 7th arr.
Telephone: 01 43 26 46 71 • Métro: Saint-Sulpice, Sevres-Babylone
Tuesday through Saturday 11am to 2pm, 3pm to 7pm
closed Sunday, Monday
carinegilson.com

AT THE AGE OF 23, CARINE GILSON SPENT HER ENTIRE SAVINGS AND BOUGHT A FORMER BRUSSELS LINGERIE ATELIER. NOT LONG after, she sold her first lingerie collection to exclusive buyers in some of Europe's largest cities. Gilson uses Lyonnaise silk and Chantilly

lace in her refined, delicate items. In a range of colors—from the palest rose to turquoise and citrine—the handmade lingerie is made to enhance a woman's figure. A pair of culottes is replete with detail, luxurious but never too frilly; a bra is intricate, but not flashy. The boutique itself, opened in 2005 in Saint-Germain, is a modern boudoir-like space with flesh-colored walls and intimate, soft lighting. Here, lingerie is pure luxury, with a price tag to match (swim suits start at 300 euros). A *sur mesure* service is available, making this truly couture lingerie.

Editions de Parfums Frédéric Malle

37, rue de Grenelle, 7th arr.
Telephone: 01 42 22 76 40 • Métro: Rue du Bac
Monday through Saturday 11am to 7pm, closed Sunday
editionsdeparfums.com

FRÉDÉRIC MALLE, GRANDSON OF THE FOUNDER OF DIOR PERFUMES, BRINGS TOGETHER THE SCENTS OF CELEBRATED fragrance creators under one roof. Malle asks each "nose" to create an ideal fragrance, granting complete freedom of expression. The perfumes are then packaged in the same minimalist-style bottles and sold exclusively in Malle shops and in select boutiques-within-boutiques. The fragrances are opulent counterpoints to the duty-free shop fragrances that are available *partout*. The experience of picking out a scent at Frederic Malle is equally unique—the staff is trained to ask specific questions (for example, "Do you wear perfume for yourself or others?" or "What are you favorite brands of clothing?") to make choosing a perfume a uniquely personal experience. Certain scents are released into floor-to-ceiling glass columns, each with a window, which allows clients to lean in and clearly smell the fragrance without wearing it. The innovative columns envelop you with the "aura" of the fragrance, to experience the scent that you would leave in your trail when wearing it. The rue de Grenelle boutique is the original boutique.

Etienne Brunel

37, rue de Grenelle, 7th arr.
Telephone: 01 45 48 26 13 • Métro: Rue du Bac
Monday 3pm to 8pm, Tuesday through Saturday
10am to 8pm, closed Sunday
etienne-brunel.com

MIREILLE ETIENNE BRUNEL STARTED HER CAREER WITH A READY-TO-WEAR LINE. IN 1997 SHE OPENED THIS SHOP THAT OFFERS one-of-a-kind wedding dresses. The fresh, light look of the dresses is surprising, and the material is even more so—the dresses are made of paper. An under-dress is made from an opaque paper that will not tear, and the overlay is a transparent light-filtering paper; both resist rain and fire, should your wedding day take an unexpected turn. The two layers combine to give an ethereal, graceful, romantic yet modern look. Each dress is a unique creation; feathers, delicate flowers, paillettes, feathers, and beads can be added according to the bride's desires. Traditional silk dresses are also on offer, also with simple silhouettes and distinctive details, always with ultra-light results. Dresses start at 2000 euros, and take several fittings to complete. After the big day, the dress can be shortened and dyed to make a cocktail dress. The shop also specializes in veils, evening dresses, corsets, and maternity dresses; fabric by the meter is available for purchase.

Muriel Grateau

37, rue de Beaune, 7th arr.
Telephone: 01 40 20 42 82 • Métro: Rue du Bac
Monday through Saturday 11am to 7pm, closed Sunday
murielgrateau.com

MURIEL GRATEAU'S MINIMALIST SHOP ON A STREET OF ART GALLERIES IS KNOWN FOR ITS IMPRESSIVE RANGE OF JEWEL-toned table linens. Simple linen napkins and tablecloths in more than one hundred colors (such as aubergine, celery, charcoal) are displayed along a long wall. A full range of dishes, tableware, and porcelain-handled flatware in simple, modern shapes in assorted muted tones complete the necessary accoutrements of a very French table. Up a short staircase at the back of the store you'll find Grateau's jewelry collection. Large carved onyx bracelets, chunky rings, and heavy cameo pieces are on display. Sensual, elegant lines and fine craftsmanship are hallmarks of the brand, which counts minimalist master Calvin Klein as a fan.

Ovale

∞

200, boulevard Saint-Germain, 7th arr.
Telephone: 01 53 63 31 11 • Métro: Saint-Germain-des-Près
Monday through Saturday 10:30am to 7:30pm, closed Sunday
ovale.com

YOU WON'T FIND ANY PINKS OR BLUES AT THIS LUXURY CONCEPT STORE FOR *BÉBÉ* IN THE HEART OF SAINT-GERMAIN. THE EXQUISITE and tasteful items presented in this shop are done in whites, tans, and browns. All items are unisex, for babies up to one year old: simple white cotton "apron" bibs, wool hats with attached scarves, fine cotton sweater sets, and little pants. Other über-chic gifts on hand include baby jewelry such as bracelets with silver or gold mini-blocks, bell-shaped rattles, and a sterling receptacle to hold the cork from baby's (or mom's!) first bottle of champagne. Winter and summer items are available all year long, allowing gift givers to buy in advance. All items—from the luxe cashmere blankets, simple bibs, and elaborate christening gowns to a sterling napkin ring—can be personalized with embroidery or engraving. Gilles Neveu, who once designed at Dior, is the talent behind the line.

Ramosport

188, boulevard Saint-Germain, 7th arr.
Telephone: 01 42 22 70 80 • Métro: Saint-Germain-des-Près
Monday 2pm to 7pm, Tuesday through
Saturday 10:30am to 7pm, closed Sunday
ramosport.com

LUXURY OUTERWEAR LINE RAMOSPORT WAS FOUNDED IN RUSSIA AT THE TURN OF THE CENTURY BY A YOUNG WOMAN WHO IMPORTED water-resistant fabric to make the jackets of the Csar's army. The business was carried on by women through four generations, moved to Paris during the Revolution, and was opened as a raincoat boutique. In the 1950s, the chic trench coats were embraced by an upscale clientele for their combination of style and practicality. Each season presents a multitude of styles, in materials such as washable suede, patent leather, and waxed cotton, perhaps in oversized prints or detailed with studs. You may find trenches and windbreakers in satin that pack wrinkle-free. The business is now owned by Italian Nicoletta Giadrossi, who periodically asks guest designers (Marcel Marongiu, Hussein Chalayan) to interpret the classic trench. Spring 2008 brings a new line designed by design team E2, featuring details such as jeweled belts, feathers, or patent trim. An accessory line with hats, umbrellas, and scarves completes the look; colors range from the classic taupe to light gray and white.

Un jour un sac

27, boulevard Raspail, 7th arr.
Telephone: 01 45 49 26 88 • Métro: Sevres-Babylone
Monday 2pm to 7pm, Tuesday through Saturday 11am to 1pm
2pm to 7pm, closed Sunday
unjourunsac.com

IN THIS SMALL BOUTIQUE IN SAINT-GERMAIN, CUSTOMERS ARE ABLE TO CUSTOMIZE THEIR OWN PURSES. CREATOR FRANCOIS RENIER HAS designed a wide array of bags and a huge assortment of handles—it is up to you to choose which combinations suit you best. The simple totes are made of paper, fabric, leather, and crocodile—in all sorts of colors and patterns; the handles, with large metal clips on the end, are available in multiple lengths, in leather, PVC, crocodile, and cotton. Customers can pick several of each component for a versatile variety of options. For fall, choose fuchsia leather handles with a black and white tweed tote, or go matchy-matchy and do silver leather with a silver woven bag. Accessories such as leather pouches and key chains are made to clip on the bags as well, for the ultimate in practicality. The bags are all made in France by artisans.

8th

Arrondissement

Cassegrain

422, rue Saint-Honoré, 8th arr.
Telephone: 01 42 60 20 08 • Métro: Madeleine
Monday through Saturday 10am to 7pm, closed Sunday
cassegrain.fr

ONE OF THE OLDEST *GRAVEURS* IN PARIS, CASSEGRAIN HAS BEEN ENGRAVING STATIONERY ITEMS SINCE 1919 IN THE SAME LOCATION on rue Saint-Honoré, using traditional copper and steel engraving blocks. The helpful staff will help you pick out the perfect *cartes de visite* and advise on how and when to use them. The thick paper exudes quality and the wooden paneled boutique embodies good taste. Clients include the *crème de la crème* of Parisian society. Customized stationery can be had in about three weeks for engraved cards (ten days for printed), both of which can be sent abroad. If your stationery box is full, check out the fine leather goods such as journals, agendas, wallets, desk accessories, and pens.

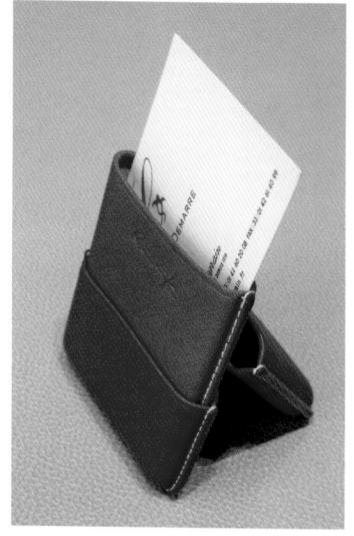

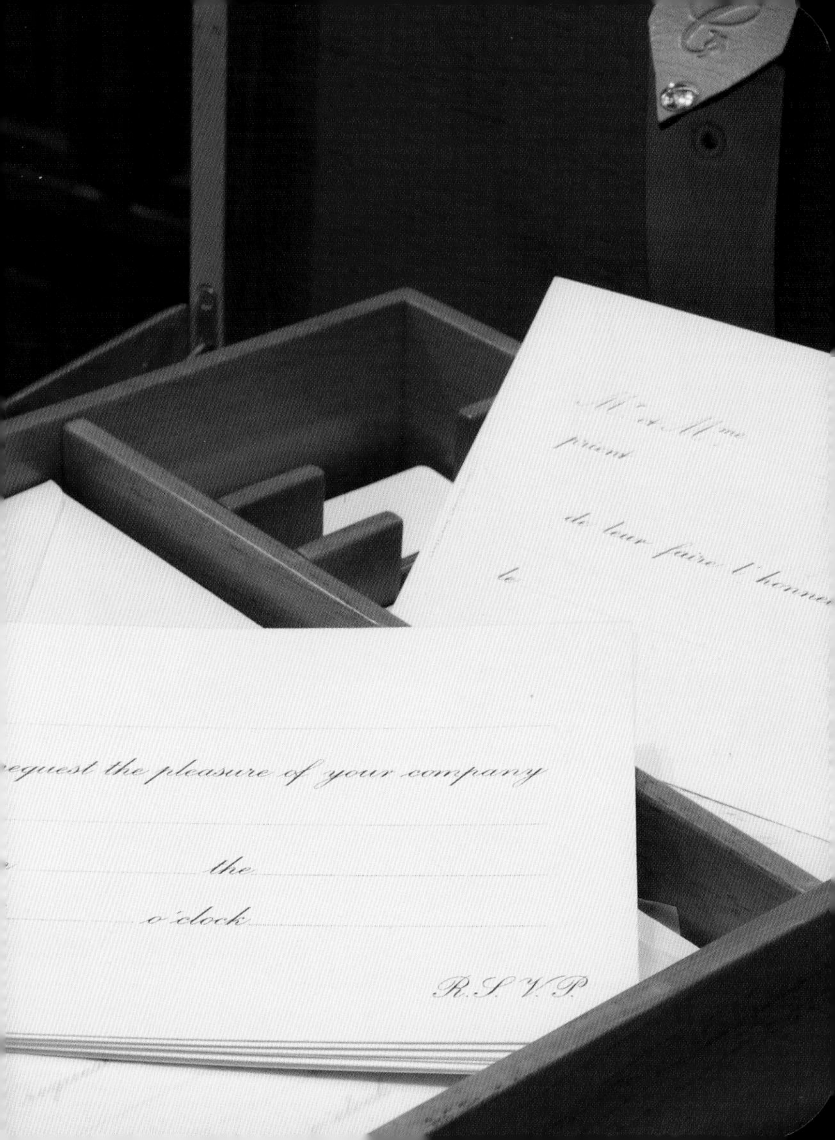

M... M...

présent

de leur faire l'honneur

le

...request the pleasure of your company

the

o'clock

R.S.V.P.

Gripoix

9, rue du Boccador, 8th arr.
Telephone: 01 56 64 09 09 • Métro: Alma-Marceau
By appointment only
gripoix.fr

OUNDED IN 1869 BY AUGUSTINE GRIPOIX, THE HOUSE ORIGI-
NALLY BECAME FAMOUS AS A MANUFACTURER OF ITS SIGNATURE
pate de verre (poured glass) jewelry pieces for Chanel, Lanvin, and
other prestigious couturiers. The artisanal process, a dying art practiced
only in a handful of Parisian ateliers, uses melted liquid glass, colored like
precious stones, which is poured into metal molds. Some of the meticu-
lously crafted pieces take several hundred hours to complete. Best known
for its whimsical natural themes, as in dragonfly and *rose de noel*
("Christmas rose") brooches, Gripoix has recently begun to update its look
and distribute jewelry under its own name. Gilles Dufour, who has worked
at Balmain, Pierre Cardin, and for fifteen years with Karl Lagerfeld at
Chanel, was brought in as creative director, to give new energy and a
younger vibe to the line. New designs include masculine silver chains with
flowers in muted colors and "bonbon" bracelets with balls of colored glass,
meant to be piled on. Long sautoir necklaces, popular in the Flapper Age,
are still a staple of the line, in 24k gold, silver, and bronze; they hang to the
floor when put on, and are meant to be looped around several times. The
house currently has a showroom, but no boutique, and receives personal
shoppers and private clients by appointment.

Maison Calavas

13 rue Royale, 8th arr.
Telephone: 01 40 07 57 57 • Métro: Madeleine, Concorde
Monday through Friday 11am to 7pm, closed Saturday, Sunday
maisoncalavas.fr

MAISON CALAVAS IS TUCKED AWAY IN A COURTYARD, AWAY FROM THE HUSTLE OF RUE ROYALE. AFTER RINGING THE BELL and being welcomed inside, one enters a stunning eighteenth-century salon, with soaring ceilings and a luxe atmosphere—the perfect background for Maison Calavas' intricate *minaudières*. These small, ornamental makeup cases are made artisanally from yellow and rose gold, crocodile skin, shagreen, sycamore wood, and other luxury materials. They are filled with custom makeup—a refillable palette of one powder, one blush, four eye shadows, and two lip colors, laid out inside the compact like a mini-mosaic. The final detail in the sleek package is a hidden drawer for brushes. By appointment, a special salon, the Ultraviolet, can be reserved for a makeup lesson or a VIP sale, or to view the limited-edition compacts made by well-known artist/creators such as Serge Amoruso and Pierre Bonnefille. Each graceful *minaudière* is small enough to pop into an oversized *sac* for day, but large enough to use as a mini-clutch at night.

Repetto

22, rue de la Paix, 8th arr.
Telephone: 01 44 71 83 12 • Métro: Opéra
Monday through Saturday 10am to 7pm, closed Sunday
repetto.com

REPETTO WAS ORIGINALLY KNOWN FOR SUPPLYING BALLET SLIPPERS AND LEOTARDS FOR THE BALLERINAS OF THE OPÉRA Garnier on the nearby place de l'Opéra, but in 1956 when Bridgette Bardot wore them in "And God Created Woman," the brand became an iconic staple of the Parisienne's wardrobe. Today, the boutique carries hundreds of versions of the classic ballet flat—in plaid, patent, satin, leather, suede, glitter, and more, in a multitude of styles, along with heeled versions for tango or cabaret dancing. In recent years, Issey Miyake, Yohji Yamamoto, and Comme des Garçons have collaborated on models. The shoes are fanned out on low, round tables, echoing the shapes of the tutus decorating the boutique, while classical music floats through the shop. The back wall displays classic pale pink ballet slippers exclusively. A large line of ballet accessories is available, with headbands, legwarmers, and leotards for girls and women, along with a small line of leather handbags.

9th
Arrondissement

Alice à Paris

64, rue Condorcet, 9th arr.
Telephone: 01 48 78 17 31 • Métro: Pigalle, Anvers
Monday 2pm to 7pm, Tuesday through Saturday
11am to 7:30pm, closed Sunday

WHEN DESIGNER GÉRALDINE BOUDAREL GAVE BIRTH TO HER DAUGHTER ALICE, ANOTHER IDEA MADE ITS DEBUT AS WELL: a line of trendy yet *classique* children's clothing. The brand, Alice à Paris, was founded four years ago, first with private sales, followed by a boutique open to the public in this trendy part of the ninth arrondissement. Inside, the clean lines of the boutique—whitewashed walls, wooden floor—echo the simple forms of the clothing. With bloomers for spring and capes for fall, the look is retro-classic with a boho twist, and oh-so-French at the same time. The line offers uncomplicated Bonpoint-ish looks in simple palettes, without the Bonpoint price tag. To keep the look fresh, basics such as t-shirts, denim, and blouses are done in small, limited series; the Liberty prints and fabric patterns change every few weeks. The line, until now only sold in Montmartre, recently opened another boutique in the sixth.

Anna Rivka

57, rue Condorcet, 9th arr.
Telephone: 01 40 23 92 84 • Métro: Pigalle, Anvers
Monday 2pm to 8pm, Tuesday through Saturday
noon to 8pm, closed Sunday

OPENED IN THE SPRING OF 2007 ON THE UP-AND-COMING RUE CONDORCET, THIS BOUTIQUE MIXES VINTAGE AND NEW—PIECES from old jewelry are remounted with new semi-precious stones to create something uncommon and unexpected. Plastic bracelets are embellished with multicolored gems, and lapis earrings get an update with 1930s pompoms attached. The *créatrice* mixes old with new; the result is distinctive and interesting, a statement in favor of inspired individuality rather than mass-produced statement pieces. The decor of the shop is along the same lines—understated pale gray walls mixed with vintage brass jewelry cases on long gray legs, tasteful and uncomplicated.

Detaille

10, rue Saint Lazare, 9th arr.
Telephone: 01 48 78 68 50 • Métro: Notre-Dame de Lorette
Monday 3pm to 7pm, Tuesday through Saturday
10am to 1:30pm, 2pm to 7pm, closed Sunday
detaille.com

ETAILLE IS TUCKED AWAY BEHIND NOTRE-DAME DE LORETTE, ON A STREET NOT FAR FROM LES GRANDS MAGASINS. THIS SMALL Parisian perfumer, founded in 1905, was reenergized by new buyers in 1990 who were inspired to recreate the brand's turn-of-the-century formulas. The petite shop looks frozen in time, lined with wooden cabinets and mirrored walls. In addition to perfumes, the line includes loose powder, lotions, skin care products, and candles. The brand is known for its "Baume Automobile," a non-greasy fluid originally formulated to protect the skin when driving in one's newfangled *voiture*; it is still available today and said to be effective against city pollution. Other well-loved products include the Sanos mask with fresh egg whites and a citrus vinegar astringent, all made with natural ingredients and without preservatives or colorants. The demure, Victorian-era packaging remains unchanged, with a cameo portrait of the original Madame Detaille in the center. The ladylike bottles make a lovely addition to your dressing table.

Karine Arabian

4, rue Papillon, 9th arr.
Telephone: 01 45 23 23 24 • Métro: Cadet, Poissonniere
Monday through Saturday 9:30am to 7pm, closed Sunday
karinearabian.com

LA MADONNE AND SCARLETT JOHANSSON ARE FANS OF HER RETRO SEXY SHOES, AS IS VANESSA PARADIS—KARINE ARABIAN IS QUICKLY becoming a hot new name in Paris and abroad. Her rue Papillon shop houses a much bigger collection than you'll find elsewhere. Arabian comes from a family of boot makers and tailors, and mastered the details of fine production while growing up. Polishing her skills at Chanel, where she oversaw accessories, she launched her own line in 2000. Arabian's shoes and bags are clean and modern, with an often interesting mix of materials and a bit of humor. The laid-back shop, with its unfinished wood floors and 1950s couch, is calm and inviting.

Ube Ule

59, rue de Condorcet, 9th arr.
Telephone: 01 45 26 93 63 • Métro: Anvers, Pigalle
Monday through Friday 9:30am to 7pm, Saturday
9:30am to 7:30pm, closed Sunday, Monday
ube-ule.com

UBE ULE TAKES ITS NAME FROM A CHILDLIKE PRONUNCIATION OF LIBELLULE, THE FRENCH WORD FOR DRAGONFLY, AND INDEED the colorful creations seem to be flying around the shop, hanging from the walls and ceiling. A multi-label boutique with garments for mother and child, the shop also sells its own line, which includes maternity clothes designed to be worn before and after the baby is born, and children's clothing up to age six. The line's creators originally started designing fun tunic tops for pregnant friends; the project evolved into a full-on shop about two years ago. Their cheerful kids items (colorful Liberty print dresses with satin ribbon ties), are a unique and bright addition to the pastel palette that remains a mainstay of Parisian childrenswear. A fun selection of toys, kids bedroom decor, creations from other designers, and baby shoes round out the collection. The entire layette line is also made in house and hand-embroidered with the dragonfly logo. Pick up a handmade sleep sack or crib bumper or have one designed to match your nursery.

Woch Dom

72, rue Condorcet, 9th arr.
Telephone: 01 53 21 09 72 • Métro: Pigalle, Saint-Georges
Monday through Saturday 11am to 8pm, closed Sunday

FROM THE OUTSIDE, THE SHOP LOOKS LIKE A NIGHTCLUB OR MAYBE EVEN AN ASIAN EATERY, WITH TINTED WINDOWS AND A black exterior. The theme continues inside, with black walls as a backdrop for a colorful assortment of vintage clothing and accessories. Rudy Cohen's collection, which comes from as close by as the *vide greniers* (yard sales) in the neighboring eighteenth arrondissement and as far away as Japan, is no hodgepodge of vintage junk, but arranged neat as a pin, by item and by color. The collection does not focus on brand names as much as it focuses on cut, style, and detail. A men's section, a rarity in vintage shops, is another welcome addition. The impeccably curated collection has quickly become a favorite, with queues often forming at lunchtime. Not surprisingly, Kirsten Dunst is a fan, as are designers from some of the big-name houses (Gucci, Marc Jacobs), who come here for inspiration.

10th
Arrondissement

Dante & Maria

3, rue de la Grange aux Belles, 10th arr.
Telephone: 01 43 43 76 46 • Métro: Republique
Tuesday through Sunday noon to 7pm
dantemaria.fr

AFTER WORKING BEHIND THE SCENES AT GIVENCHY AND KAR-INE ARABIAN, DESIGNER AGNÈS SINELLE STARTED HER OWN line of accessible, affordable jewelry in a boutique named after her grandparents. This new location, a former laboratory, is the perfect setting for this designer, who considers her jewelry atelier a place to experiment with unique pieces. The boutique carries its own line—each piece one-of-a-kind and made by hand—as well as other pieces from a few small creators, all in small, limited editions. Most of the jewelry is silver with semi-precious and natural stones, in simple, sweet styles with dangly charms and gems. Motifs such as keys, butterflies, and flowers influence the line, and the calm, feminine boutique seems like just the right place to pop in to buy yourself a little gift while picking out one for a friend. (And with the maximum price being 200 euros, it is *tout a fait raisonnable*.)

11th
Arrondissement

Anne Willi

⸻ ∞ ⸻

13, rue Keller, 11th arr.
Telephone: 01 48 06 74 06 • Métro: Bastille
Monday 2pm to 6pm, Tuesday through Saturday
11:30am to 8pm, closed Sunday
annewilli.com

ANNE WILLI STARTED HER CAREER AFTER FASHION SCHOOL BY MAKING COSTUMES FOR A MODERN DANCE TROUPE; THE movement and flexibility that she focused on then are still part of her collection today. Willi opened her Paris boutique on rue Keller in 1998; it was the first boutique on the street that is now filled with a bevy of trendy shops. Her collection is comprised of limited-edition pieces with unconventional cuts. Many of the pieces can be worn in various ways—a dress with a long sash can be tied differently, a skirt is reversible. The poetic and architectural line mixes materials and tones, feminine and masculine elements, comfort and originality. In 2002, she launched a children's line (for ages zero to six); the adorable mini-me looks can be worn with or without the matching mom version.

Des Petits Hauts

5, rue Keller, 11th arr.
Telephone: 01 43 38 14 39 • Métro: Ledru-Rollin
Tuesday-Friday 11:30am to 7pm, Saturday 11:30am to 8pm
closed Sunday
despetitshauts.com

IN 1999, SISTERS KATIA AND VANESSA SANCHEZ CREATED THE LINE CALLED "SOME LITTLE TOPS" WITH A COLLECTION OF FUNKY TOPS with fun details such as a small embroidered picture or an interesting sleeve or hem. The shirts are as appealing as bright candies, cute without being overly trendy, with simple shapes. In winter the line expands to bring out more heavy knits (sweaters, little jackets, sweater dresses), and in summer you'll find tees, tanks, and sweater sets in fine, layer-able knits. Look closely to find the tiny dangling star medallion, the brand's trademark, which is often sewn near the hem. The shop carries accessories from other young creators to help you complete the look, including gloves, scarves, and jewelry. The brand now counts three bubble gum–pink shops in Paris; the rue Keller is the original shop and the largest.

Les Fleurs

3, Passage de la Bonne Graine, 11th arr.
Telephone: 01 43 55 12 94 • Métro: Ledru-Rollin
Tuesday-Friday 3pm to 7:30pm, Saturday 11:30am to 7:30pm
closed Sunday, Monday
lesfleurs.canalblog.com

FANS OF GIRLY, FLOWERY THINGS WILL ADORE THE COLLECTION OF GIFT AND HOME ITEMS AT LES FLEURS, IN THE COBBLESTONE Passage de la Bonne Graine, not far from the Bastille. This charming and quaint little shop offers butterfly nets, little bijoux, change purses, cute notebooks and upbeat accessories. Owner Lucie makes one-of-a-kind items, such as vintage purses embellished with lace and flowers, and *tabourets* (stools) decorated with vintage French comics. She sells items from more than sixty designers as well, most of them French. Brands like Dentelle Gourmande (little woven bracelets and headbands, packaged like bonbons), Petit Jour (cardboard mini-*valises* and waxed-cloth, polka-dot bags), and Les Touristes (orchid-printed journals and makeup bags) are all on hand. Shelves are filled with a poetic and playful assortment of metal tins, dainty glassware, paper fans, and objects featuring wood, ribbon, flowers, metal, birds, feathers, and butterflies.

Gaëlle Barré

17, rue Keller, 11th arr.
Telephone: 01 43 14 63 02 • Métro: Bastille
Monday 2pm to 7pm, Tuesday through Saturday 11:30am to 8pm
closed Sunday
gaellebarre.com

GAELLE BARRÉ'S POETIC, FEMININE COLLECTION OF CLOTHING FOR WOMEN AND CHILDREN IS ON DISPLAY IN HER SIMPLE SPACE WITH blond wooden fittings and retro mannequin heads; the designer works on her collection in the back. The shop, started in 1998 after a career in couture, then in prêt-à-porter, is a favorite address for Parisians in the know and is also very popular in Japan. The line? Dresses, dresses, and more dresses. Ethereal, retro-inspired summer frocks are often designed in a mix of prints—stripes with florals, for example—perhaps with contrasting piping. In winter the dresses are paired with funky shrugs, cardigans, vests, and muffs. The children's line, for boys and girls up to age eight, is also focused on patterns, mixing prints and adding details such as rickrack and piping. Barré also designs unique wedding dresses, by appointment, made on the premises.

Lilli Bulle

3, rue de la Forge Royale, 11th arr.
Telephone: 01 43 73 71 63 • Métro: Faidherbe-Chaligny
Tuesday through Friday 10am to 1:30pm, 3pm to 7pm
Saturday 11:30am to 7pm, closed Sunday, Monday
lillibulle.com

LILLI BULLE'S LIME GREEN FAÇADE INSTANTLY LET YOU KNOW YOU ARE IN A CREATIVE, HAPPY SPACE. THIS INSPIRED CHILDREN'S SHOP showcases more than eighty different brands, mainly small French *créateurs*, such as 180 grammes, WOWO, and more. Anne-Christelle Beauvois' two young sons are her testing ground—all the clothing she carries must be durable, practical, and washable, as well as stylish and *amusant*. The age range offered is zero to twelve years old, but adults will find all sorts of goodies as well—check out the lovely fine wool polka-dot scarves by Bellerose, the felt medallion brooches by Miaow, or the adorable mini-cape by Anomalies (made for children but often borrowed by *maman* as well!). A large part of the collection is available on her blog/shop, along with fun commentary about the designers. Beauvois will gladly help you shop for your *enfant* or find a witty *cadeau*.

Marci N'oum

1, rue Keller, 11th arr.
Telephone: 01 42 33 06 44 • Métro: Bastille
Monday 2pm to 7pm, Tuesday through Saturday 11am to 7pm
closed Sunday
marcinoum.fr

CREATED FIVE YEARS AGO BY ISABELLE AND JEAN CLAUDE N'DOUMBÉ, THE MARCI N'OUM WOMEN'S CLOTHING LINE IS A BOHEMIAN MIX with an urban influence. The couple reinterprets basics, adding in a mix of interesting fabrics and details, and the result is something eccentric and very French. The boutique, with its concrete floor and velvet curtains, is the perfect setting for their sophisticated boho look, influenced by world travel. The summer line is full of eye-catching color and pattern, and the winter line is more citified, with grays, black and neutrals, still with a mix of patterns and unusual cuts. Following the lead of other designers on this street (Gaelle Barré and Anne Willi), the couple created a kid's collection, Baby N'oum, (for two- to eight-year olds), following the birth of their child a few years ago.

Philippe Roucou

30, rue de Charonne, 11th arr.
Telephone: 01 43 38 81 16 • Métro: Ledru-Rollin
Tuesday through Saturday 11:30am to 7:30pm, closed Sunday, Monday
philipperoucou.com

PHILIPPE ROUCOU, WHO HAILS FROM MARSEILLE, OPENED HIS FIRST BOUTIQUE IN 2002 AFTER DESIGNING ACCESSORIES FOR Etienne Brunel and for friend and muse Miki Mialy. In his minimalist boutique near Bastille, Roucou displays leather goods that are slightly avant garde, ranging from classic to edgy. Inspired by the 1970s, icons such as Grace Kelly, and well-established leather goods brands, each Roucou collection tells a new "story," changing colors, leathers, and volumes. A recent collection included large leather totes named "Edie Sedgwick" and small clutches with an integrated combination lock called "Palace." Materials include python, long-haired goat, and supple Italian leathers. The line includes overnight bags, clutches, gloves, scarves, and belts. Funky meets elegant might just describe this look, for those in search of a unique, urban bag.

Wall Design

25, rue de la Forge Royale, 11th arr.
Telephone: 01 43 48 30 24 • Métro: Faidherbe-Chaligny
Monday, Thursday, Friday 10:30am to 1:30pm, 3pm to 7pm, Saturday
11am to 7pm, closed Sunday, Tuesday, Wednesday
walldesign.fr

A GRAPHIC LITTLE BOUTIQUE SET ON A NARROW STREET NEAR BASTILLE, WALLDESIGN FACES A SMALL NEIGHBORHOOD park—a source of inspiration. Since June 2004, Fabienne and Olivier Lescloupe have been promoting a new sort of interior design—stickers as wall art. The pair teams up with artists to make giant adhesive designs to decorate living spaces, con-

sidered "ready-to-make" not "ready-made" artwork. There is a certain degree of interpretation that goes into the process—the customer not only chooses the pattern, but decides where to put it on the wall and how to arrange it. The French-made collections range from the flowery "Jardin d'Eden" to "My Wall" (large letters) to the trees of "Fôret Domestique" and the angular "Dessins Chimériques." Designs can be customized to suit the size and proportion of a space;

a design or text can also be custom to made. Detailed directions on the website describe how to apply the designs, and a simulation on the site lets customers play around with patterns and colors before making a choice.

12ᵗʰ
Arrondissement

Louison

20, rue Saint-Nicolas, 12th arr.
Telephone: 01 43 44 02 62 • Métro: Ledru-Rollin
Tuesday through Saturday 11:30am to 7pm, closed Sunday, Monday

AWAY FROM THE HUSTLE AND BUSTLE OF FAUBOURG SAINT-ANTOINE, ON A SIDE STREET IN THE BASTILLE NEIGHBORHOOD, Louison attracts trendy neighborhood patrons as well as international clients. Husband and wife team Jacques Choi and wife Agnès (he used to design accessories for Celine) started the brand in 2001—they work and live just across the courtyard from the boutique. Their famous *paillette* (glitter) bags are supple, lightweight, completely lighthearted, and come in a range of brights and neutrals, in shapes such as a small duffle, tote, yoga bag, and even a disco-bright garment bag. They also offer modern and sleek leather bags, and accessories such as dog collars, luggage tags, and a small line of shoes, in interesting metallic leathers. This quiet shop has a stellar product that continues to turn heads in Paris.

Valérie Salacroux

69, rue Crozatier, 12th arr.
Telephone: 01 46 28 79 09 • Métro: Faidherbe-Chaligny
Monday through Friday noon to 7pm, Saturday 10am to 2pm
closed Sunday
valeriesalacroux.com

OPENED FOR JUST ABOUT A YEAR NOW, VALÉRIE SALACROUX'S ACCESSORY BOUTIQUE, ON AN UNDISTINGUISHED STREET NEAR the frenzied Marché d'Aligre street market, is already a destination for those in the know. Salacroux spent time designing shoes for Miu Miu, Prada, and Balenciaga before setting off to start her own brand. Inspired by her roots in the Basque region of France, her sandal collection in summer is very classic—flat leather soles with metallic wraparound straps that snap on the ankle, snakeskin wedges with cork soles. For fall, she updates the classic ballerina flat in cobra. You'll find python, crocodile, and bull leather across the collection as well as more traditional leathers. Artisanal craftsmanship is evident in every piece. Overall, the style is very Parisienne: feminine, but not frilly; classic. Salacroux also has a collection of bags, also using unusual leathers and hides, with chain or twill straps.

16th Arrondissement

Noël

1, avenue Pierre 1er de Serbie, 16th arr.
Telephone: 01 40 70 14 63 • Métro: Iena
Monday through Saturday 10:30am to 7pm
noel.fr

THE LUXURY LINEN BRAND NOEL WAS ESTABLISHED AT THE TURN OF THE CENTURY, AND ACHIEVED LUXURY STATUS IN THE 20s AND 30s, when it was used by sophisticated hostesses at the Elysée Palace in Paris and in New York City by society luminaries such as Helena Rubenstein. Noel is also credited with providing the hand-embroidered linens for Prince Charles' cradle. The shop changed hands in the 1980s after Madame Noel's death, and again in the 90s, but it remains true to its roots as a luxury embroidery house. Everything in the shop is embroidered, from formal table linens to towel sets, layette items, pajamas, and bed linens. Linen, organdy, damask, cotton, and percale are used, and embroidery themes range from little chickens or dolphins that grace a baby bib to the silver embroidered "constellation" tablecloth that was decorated with 2,000 stars to mark the millennium.

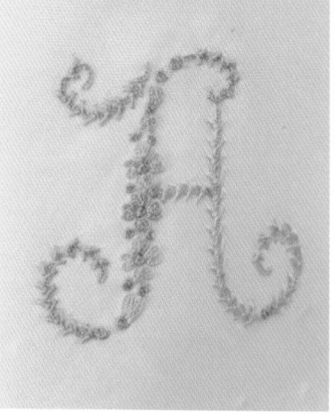

The venerable house has more than 13,000 designs in its archives, dating back to 1883; new designs are constantly being created as well. Many of the products can be made to measure, and in-house designers can create a custom monogram, a family crest, or an exclusive design. Vintage heirlooms from Noel can be matched, and linen care services for fine linens of all brands are available.

Princesse Tam-Tam

2, rue Guichard, 16th arr.
Telephone: 01 42 15 18 85 • Métro: La Muette
Monday 1:30pm to 7pm, Tuesday through Saturday 10am to 7pm
closed Sunday
princessetam-tam.com

THE PRINCESSE TAM-TAM LINE OF LINGERIE IS A FUN, RETRO-INSPIRED LINE THAT WILL BE EASIER ON YOUR WALLET THAN WHAT'S OFFERED at many of the other Parisian lingerie shops. The lingerie here is an accessible luxury. Flirty, but not immature, the refined color palette and fun themes (think dainty fruits, vintage comic book cats) and details (simple lace, decorative buttons) and fabrics ranging from Liberty floral prints to bright graphics make sure there is something for everyone. The brand was started twenty years ago by a pair of sisters who wanted to try something different—printed, colorful lingerie was unheard of until this duo came out with their creative take. The shops carry *corseterie* (bras, panties), swimwear, and accessories, as well as cute lounge- and sleepwear, in their famous demure pinup-style boutiques, which are sexy but never vulgar.

18th
Arrondissement

Belle de Jour

7, rue Tardieu, 18th arr.
Telephone: 01 46 06 15 28 • Métro: Anvers, Abbesses
Monday through Saturday 10:30am to 1pm, 2pm to 7pm, closed Sunday

MONSIEUR SCHALBURG, A COLLECTOR AT HEART, HAS A COLLECTION OF NINETEENTH- AND TWENTIETH-CENTURY PIECES that might well be of museum quality. In business for twenty-five years at the *pied* of the Sacré Coeur, sandwiched between two souvenir shops, the boutique contains a distinctive array of all things perfume-related: vintage perfume ads, atomizers, accessories for the vanity, and more. Perfume is not sold here, however, so if you purchase a *flaçon* to decorate your vanity or as a gift, you must head elsewhere for the perfect scent; here you can only buy the receptacle.

Dognin Paris

4, rue des Gardes, 18th arr.
Telephone: 01 44 92 32 16 • Métro: Barbes-Rochechouart
Tuesday through Saturday 10am to 6pm, closed Sunday, Monday
dogninparis.com

THIS OFF-THE-BEATEN-PATH SHOP ON THE UP-AND-COMING RUE DES GARDES HAS BAGS, BAGS, AND MORE BAGS MANUFACTURED IN A workshop in the hills of Montmartre. Founded in 2000 by Luc Dognin, formerly a designer at Celine, and Rafik Mahiout, who manages the business, the line focuses on comfortable and simple bags with lots of pockets and compartments in myriad colors. Every season, new styles are designed to suit a woman's daily life—bags for the city, an evening out, travel, or work. Some seasons the collection is based on a shape, such as the duffle, or a classic 50s silhouette; sometimes, it is based on a fashion item like the corset. The line can be humorous, and is always very imaginative with a touch of poetry, but the clean lines and nice finishes make it accessible to a traditional customer. The light bags often have extendable handles that make them practical *en plus*. Several of the bags were featured on "Sex & the City," but other than that, the line remains relatively unknown stateside.

Ebano

27, rue Durantin, 18th arr.
Telephone: 01 42 51 71 29 • Métro: Abbesses
Tuesday through Sunday 2pm to 8pm, closed Monday
ebano.fr

S HE'S ITALIAN, HE'S SENEGALESE, THEY HAVE LIVED IN NEW YORK CITY, AND, NOW IN PARIS, MILENA PEACE AND HAMATH SALL HAVE founded the brand Ebano ("ebony" in Italian). Using wood and precious and non-precious metals, their sleek, unisex jewelry line has a hard edge that is popular with a certain alternative clientele. The edgy, strong look is not for the faint of heart; the clean lines and simple shapes definitely command a presence. The couple also works with clients to create *sur mesure* jewelry items and a small line of furniture. There are lovely, hollowed and polished ebony branches that become vases, and curvy, sculptural metal pieces that become side tables. Their diminutive boutique, just slightly off the tourist circuit in the eighteenth arrondissement, was formerly a hat atelier. And when the couple set up shop, they found a *carte de visite*, revealing that long ago, the address had also been a jeweler—a sure sign that Ebano had taken root in the right place.

Gaspard de la Butte

10 bis, rue Yvonne Le Tac, 18th arr.
Telephone: 01 42 55 99 40 • Métro: Abbesses
Tuesday through Saturday 10am to 7pm, Sunday 2pm to 7pm
closed Monday
gasparddelabutte.com

MARKED ONLY BY A RED-TILED MOSAIC ON THE SIDEWALK—WITH NO OTHER SIGN HANGING OUT FRONT—GASPARD DE la Butte is one of those shops you might miss if you weren't looking for it. The tiny shop carries clothing for babies, children, and women, in Catherine Malaure's simple, colorful style. The designer started with a kid's line years ago, and after years of hearing that the mothers shopping in the boutique wanted the same looks in bigger sizes, she created a line for women as well. The look is slightly vintage but cute and crafty, with feminine shapes for mom and simple, funky looks for kids. The small boutique is all white with touches of retro chic wallpaper, a quaint setting for the colorful duds in this shop on a winding street in Montmartre.

Géraldine Valluet

5, rue Houdon, 18th arr.
Telephone: 01 42 52 29 63 • Métro: Pigalle
Monday through Saturday 10am to 8pm, Sunday 2pm to 8pm
atelier-geraldine-valluet-paris.com

WALKING INTO THE LARGE SHOP THAT IS GERALDINE VALLUET'S JEWELRY BOUTIQUE AND ATELIER, YOU HAVE A SENSE OF TAKING a deep breath—the calm boutique at the bottom of Montmartre is swathed in pale lavenders and blues, and the cloud-covered floor instantly tells you that you are in a creative space. Mini display cases

surround the room, with a special one put at child's eye level for her children's jewelry line, Fée d'Amour. The handmade collections contain a mixed style—definitely romantic, but also partly classic, partly rock 'n' roll. Some items are purely costume jewelry, some are semi-precious stones, and the selection ranges from a simple necklace with a pendant to a full-on dangly pearl concoction. Valluet creates two collections a year (and items *sur mesure*), inspired by colors in nature, perhaps a book character, a favorite object, or a poem. The result is girly and romantic, and well–thought out—Géraldine considers jewelry a sensual experience, so she considers its contact with the skin as she creates it.

L'Objet qui Parle

86, rue des Martyrs, 18th arr.
Telephone: 06 09 67 05 30 • Métro: Pigalle
Daily 1pm to 6:30pm

YOU'LL FIND THIS TINY CUBBYHOLE OF AN ANTIQUE SHOP ON A LITTLE STREET IN MONTMARTRE THAT IS LINED WITH INTERESTING SHOPS. In this treasure trove you'll find mismatched candlesticks, vintage postcards, and *café au lait* bowls. Keep looking and you'll discover shelves stacked with gorgeous paper-thin glassware, sunburst mirrors, and stuffed birds, all of which find a comfortable home in this quaint, hole-in-the-wall boutique. Antique junk looks chic here. If you're after a country-house look, this place is a great start. If nothing else, the eclectic shop will give you ideas for decoration and make you long to own your own *maison de campagne*.

Index

~~~~~

20 sur 20 • 19

Adelline • 109
Alexandra Sojfer • 110
Alice à Paris • 160
Anna Rivka • 161
Anne Willi • 169
Anthony Peto • 56
Les Archives de la Presse • 60
L'Argenterie de Turenne • 83
Assouline • 112
Astier de Villatte • 20
Atelier Jean Rousseau • 24
Au Petit Bonheur de Chance • 85

ba&sh • 64
Belle de Jour • 187
Black'Up • 27
Blanc d'Ivoire • 113
Bois de Rose • 114
La Boutique du Palais Royale • 29
La Bovida • 30
Brontibay Paris • 88
By Terry • 31

Canzi • 89
Carabosse • 90
Carine Gilson • 141
Cassegrain • 152
Causse • 32
Christian Louboutin • 33
Cire Trudon • 115
La Compagnie de Provence Marseille • 118
Claudie Pierlot • 34
Comptoir des Cotonniers • 119
Côté Bastide • 107

Dante & Maria • 167
Des Petits Hauts • 170
Detaille • 162
Dognin Paris • 192
Dominique Picquier • 65

Ebano • 193
L'Eclaireur • 35
Editions de Parfums Frédéric Malle • 143
Egle Bespoke • 36
Entrée des Fournisseurs • 93
Etat Libre d'Orange • 66

Etienne Brunel • 144

Les Fleurs • 171

Gabrielle Geppert • 37
Gaëlle Barré • 172
Gaspard de la Butte • 194
Géraldine Valluet • 195
Gripoix • 156

Isaac Reina • 69

Jay Ahr • 38
JC Martinez • 120

K. Jacques • 96
Karine Arabian • 163
Karine Dupont • 121

Lafont • 42
Laguiole • 43
Lemaire • 70
Librarie de la Mode • 44
Lilli Bulle • 173

Lobato • 97
Lotta & Djossou • 98
Louison • 179
Lydia Courteille • 45

Maison Calavas • 157
Maison de Vacances • 46
Marci N'oum • 174
Marie Papier • 122
Marie Puce • 126
Matières à réflexion • 74
Metal Pointu's • 48
Les Mille Feuilles • 75
Mis en Demeure • 128
Le Mont Saint-Michel • 49
Muriel Grateau • 145

N. Villaret • 129
Nadine Delepine • 130
Nicole Lehmann • 99
Noël • 182

L'Objet qui Parle • 198
Les Olivades • 131

Oona L'Ourse • 132

Ovale • 146

....

Paule Ka • 50

Petite Mademoiselle • 76

La Petite Robe Noire • 51

Philippe Roucou • 175

Pierre Corthay • 58

Pierre Frey Accessories • 133

Princesse Tam-Tam • 185

....

Quidam de Revel • 78

....

Ramosport • 147

Repetto • 158

Robert le Héros • 79

....

Sabbia Rosa • 135

Sabre • 136

Les Salons du Palais Royale
    Shiseido-Serge Lutens • 54

Sandro • 100

Sentou • 101

Servane Gaxotte • 137

Skeen+ • 102

Swildens • 80

....

Tara Jarmon • 138

Titli • 81

....

Ube Ule • 164

Un jour un sac • 150

....

Valérie Salacroux • 180

Vannina Vesperini • 139

....

WallDesign • 176

Woch Dom • 165

....

Xuan-Thu Nguyen • 103

....

Yukiko • 104

Index of Shops by Type

Accessories

20 sur 20 • 19
Atelier Jean Rousseau • 24
Brontibay Paris • 88
Dominque Picquier • 65
Karine Dupont • 121
Louison • 179
Matières à réflexion • 74
Nadine Delepine • 130
Nicole Lehmann • 99
Petite Mademoiselle • 76
Robert le Héros • 79

Art

JC Martinez • 120
L'Objet qui Parle • 198

Bags

Brontibay Paris • 88
Dognin Paris • 192
Isaac Reina • 69
Karine Arabian • 163
Karine Dupont • 121
Louison • 179
Matieres à réflexion • 74
Nicole Lehmann • 99

Philippe Roucou • 175
Un jour un sac • 150

Books

Assouline • 112
Les Archives de la Presse • 60
Librarie de la Mode • 44

Candles

Cire Trudon • 115

Clothing (Children's)

Alice à Paris • 160
Anne Willi • 169
ba&sh • 64
Bois de Rose • 114
Carabosse • 90
Comptoir des Cotonniers • 119
Gaspard de la Butte • 194
Lilli Bulle • 173
Marci N'oum • 174
Marie Puce • 126
Oona l'Ourse • 132
Ovale • 146
Ube Ule • 164

Clothing (Men's)

Anthony Peto • 56
L'Eclaireur • 35
Eglé Bespoke • 36
Lemaire • 70
Matieres à réflexion • 74
Skeen + • 102
Woch Dom • 165

Clothing (Women's)

Anne Willi • 169
ba&sh • 64
Claudie Pierlot • 34
Comptoir des Cotonniers • 119
L'Eclaireur • 35
Etienne Brunel • 144
Gaëlle Barré • 172
Gaspard de la Butte • 194
Jay Ahr • 38
Le Mont Saint-Michel • 49
Des Petits Hauts • 170
La Petite Robe Noir • 51
Marci N'oum • 174
Paule Ka • 50
Ramosport • 147
Sandro • 100
Swildens • 80
Tara Jarmon • 138
Xuan-Thu Nguyen • 103

Cosmetics & Beauty

BlackUp • 27
By Terry • 31
Canzi • 89
La Compagnie de Provence
    Marseille • 118
Côté Bastide • 107
Maison Calavas • 157
Skeen + • 102

Eyeglasses

Lafont • 42

Gloves

Causse • 32

Hats

Anthony Peto • 56

Home Decor

L'Argenterie de Turenne • 83
Astier de Villatte • 20
Blanc d'Ivoire • 113
Côté Bastide • 107
Dominque Picquier • 65
Les Fleurs • 171
Les Mille Feuilles • 75
Les Olivades • 131
L'Objet qui Parle • 198
Maison de Vacances • 46
Mis en Demeure • 128
N. Villaret • 129

Pierre Frey Accessoires • 133

Robert le Héros • 79

Sentou • 101

WallDesign • 176

Jewelry

20 sur 20 • 19

Adelline • 109

Anna Rivka • 161

Dante & Maria • 167

Ebano • 193

Geraldine Valluet • 195

Gripoix • 156

Lotta & Djoussou • 98

Lydia Courteille • 45

Metal Pointu's • 48

Nadine Delepine • 130

Petite Mademoiselle • 76

Servane Gaxotte • 137

Titli • 81

Kitchen

Au Petit Bonheur de Chance • 85

Laguiole • 43

La Bovida • 30

Sabre • 136

Linens

Muriel Grateau • 145

N. Villaret • 129

Noël • 182

Lingerie

Carine Gilson • 141

Princesse Tam-Tam • 185

Sabbia Rosa • 135

Vannina Vesperini • 139

Notions

Entree des Founisseurs • 93

Perfume

Belle de Jour • 187

Côté Bastide • 107

Detaille • 162

Editions de Parfums
    Frédéric Malle • 143

Etat Libre d'Orange • 66

Les Salons du Palais Royal
    Shiseido-Serge Lutens • 54

Shoes

Christian Louboutin • 33

Karine Arabian • 163

K. Jacques • 96

Lobato • 97